FIVE @ FIFTY

FIVE @ FIFTY
BRAD FRASER

PLAYWRIGHTS CANADA PRESS
TORONTO

PLAYWRIGHTS CANADA PRESS
The Canadian Drama Publisher
202-269 Richmond St. W., Toronto, ON M5V 1X1
416.703.0013 • info@playwrightscanada.com • playwrightscanada.com

Playwrights Canada Press acknowledges the financial support of the Government of Canada through the Canada Book Fund and the Canada Council for the Arts, and of the Province of Ontario through the Ontario Arts Council and the Ontario Media Development Corporation, for our publishing activities.

Canada Council Conseil des Arts   ONTARIO ARTS COUNCIL
for the Arts   du Canada   CONSEIL DES ARTS DE L'ONTARIO

Canada   Ontario
Ontario Media Development
Corporation

Cover design by DC Hillier
Book design by Blake Sproule

LIBRARY AND ARCHIVES CANADA CATALOGUING IN PUBLICATION
Fraser, Brad, 1959-
        5 @ 50 / Brad Fraser.

A play.
Issued also in electronic formats.
ISBN 978-1-77091-087-4

        I. Title. II. Title: Five at fifty.

PS8561.R294F58 2012   C812'.54   C2012-904493-8

First edition: August 2012
Printed and bound in Canada by Marquis Book Printing, Montreal

For all the codependent enablers
and their addicts.

INTRODUCTION

I was in auditions for my play *True Love Lies* at the Factory Theatre in Toronto. There was one part for a woman in her mid-forties. The day we were reading for that character was like a parade of actresses out of my theatrical past. One after another they filed in. Their interest in the part and their commitment to giving their best reading were palpable. Some of them were keyed so high I would ask them to stop partway through their first reading, tell them to take a moment to breathe and relax, then start again.

In talking to them after the readings it became clear what the problem was. These amazing women, most of whom had resumes filled with memorable work and numerous awards, hadn't been acting much. As they matured the parts started to dry up and those jobs that had sustained them both artistically and professionally became fewer and farther between. So every time there was a call for an audition, that audition took on a new significance.

I realized the next play I wrote would have to take some steps to alleviate this problem because it seemed terribly unfair that so much talent was being squandered, forced to move out of the arts and on to other things, when most of these women were now capable of producing the most convincing, imaginative and nuanced work of their careers. And that was how I was impregnated with what was then known as *Interventing Sylvia Fairfax*.

I'd decided it would be a show with all female actors and would be about the relationships women have with one another, a subject I'd always found fascinating with the women in my extended family and with my many girl friends over the years. I began to listen to women's voices more intently. I became a voyeur, an eavesdropper, a spy on the world of the ladies, and I was amazed to discover how little I truly knew about one half of the world's population, what their concerns were, how they saw the world and were seen in return. My interest in classic actresses and their films gave me an entire repertoire of archetypes that were both inspired and insipid. *A Woman's View: How Hollywood Spoke to Women 1930–1960* by the brilliant film critic and scholar Jeanine Basinger was ingenious in decoding and illuminating the many strengths and flaws with the film industry's treatment of actresses and the characters they create and in illustrating how pervasive the lessons they taught were to their target audience.

I used social media to seek out female voices of all kinds in order to learn more about women in their middle-age. What were they most concerned with? What were their bodies doing? How had their needs and feelings changed as they experienced the aging process and menopause? I gave everyone I approached the option of speaking privately or in a more public forum. Most of them chose the public forum. We talked about dying menstrual cycles, grown children, long-term relationships, drug regimes and so much more. Many volunteered painful, personal information freely and with good humour. I owe each of them a great debt and their concerns, advice and support permeate this script.

I could see the traps. Being a gay man may have given me a rapport with many women that allows for a sometimes shocking honesty, but that rapport also brings the danger of creating characters who are female but just gay-influenced enough to become slightly more convincing drag queens. While such characters are very popular with men and women — on TV, film and stage — they are not, to me at least, authentic and I didn't want to be accused of writing such characters. I have also, on occasion, been accused of being "too hard" on my female characters — I'm sure none of the characters of any sex I was writing early in my career were as convincing as they would become as I matured — and I often felt that some people made that accusation not because I was particularly hard on the female characters, but because I was equally hard on the female characters as I was the male characters, and that sort of equality isn't something such personalities are really comfortable with, no matter how loudly they might protest otherwise — but I wanted these characters to be as genuine as they were entertaining. I was also interested in the difficulty of writing characters that were not only the same sex but also the same age and basic economic class and still keep them contrasted and interesting. While immersed in the writing of this script I discovered how both liberating and revealing it can be to write characters you have no physical connection to at all. Speaking and thinking in the voices of women allowed me to explore and reveal things that most men, even gay men, are not encouraged to dwell on.

Like so many of my plays, it took a single event in my life for the last piece of the puzzle to fall into place and lead to the final gelling of the plot. Just before embarking on this project I was forced to face the realities of addiction and codependency and the negative effects of both with a long-term couple I had known for most of my life. Seeing what alcohol was doing to both of them — despite the fact only one drank — was too much to put up with and, after a clumsy and ultimately too emotional and negative attempt at an intervention, I was forced to say goodbye to them. From that experience I realized that the play would be about friendship, addiction and moving on. The fact all the characters would be female was no longer an issue, they were simply characters in a story, just like in any other play I'd written.

Originally the show was conceived as a vehicle for Sylvia and Tricia's characters, with the others playing supporting roles, but only a couple scenes into it that began to change. As each of the characters came into focus and their voices began to emerge they started to argue with me as I wrote. "If she gets a monologue why can't I have one? How come she gets all of the funny lines? I'm going to want a costume change too, you know." It was crazy. They were taking over and I realized that what they wanted was a more democratic show, a shared experience for all of the characters, a showcase for everyone. The show still had a focus but it was the strength of these characters' voices that changed it from what I'd originally planned to what it eventually became.

The first draft was three acts, about one hundred and sixty pages and, quite rightly, horrified everyone who read it. Thankfully Braham Murray, then–artistic director of the Royal Exchange Theatre in Manchester, England, saw enough potential to commit to a two-day reading/workshop. I was equally grateful that Toronto dramaturgical treasure Iris Turcott was willing to give me a very blunt but constructive assessment of the play's strengths and weaknesses, which led to a major rewrite and edit, bringing the piece down to a much more manageable length and thematically clean draft. The only sticking point was the title, which Braham and the marketing team at the RX found challenging. After much to and fro-ing—I've often changed play titles at the last minute—I decided to replace the name Sylvia with Olivia as Edward Albee already had a title with that name in it and came up with the more timely *Five @ Fifty*.

The show opened a year later at the RX with an amazing cast and design team. Having apparently reached that point in my career where my plays are no longer developed by theatres but simply judged either worthy of production or not, there wasn't a lot of workshopping or public reading of the play. I did some rewrites and many cuts during rehearsal but, production pressures being what they are, some issues were never resolved. A poetic opening with each character listing what they were addicted to was cut after the first rather yawny preview, but I never quite found a way to reconcile a matching poetic bit at the end before we opened. I found it hard to watch the previews with an audience. As I later confessed on Facebook, "I felt like everyone was looking at my vagina."

To be fair, the script was close but not quite there. The story and characters were there, all of the events, the mood, etc., but the balance, the flavour, wasn't quite harmonious yet. There were parts where too much was being said and other areas where not enough was being said. The ending still wasn't working. These were all things that demanded a public reaction to repair, and the lack of development was deeply felt. Once a show's open and running further changes are, quite rightly, not encouraged. I flew back to Canada two days after opening. It had a very successful run.

The script, review quotes, box office reports and other enticements went out to theatres all across Canada and America. So far no one has picked up *Five @ Fifty* for production. I organized a sort of underground, guerrilla-style, invite-only, actors-working-for-free reading of the show that forced me to revisit the script and do all of the detailed alchemy required to make a play work better. The reading was wonderful and the positive response from the audience was palpable. It was this reading that allowed me to find the final scene of the show, which dispensed with the now incongruous poetic bit, and to come to this final version of the script.

I'm a bit baffled why a show about the largest group of people who make up the theatre-going audience hasn't managed to find another production. When I asked a female AD in Canada why

she wouldn't program the play she said it "Wasn't in their mandate." When I asked whether her mandate excluded plays about
women, lesbian-ish sexuality or alcoholism she simply shrugged
and smiled. Braham Murray was blunter in his assessment when
he wrote me, "Men don't give a shit and women don't trust it because it's written by you."

I hope her mandate changes and I hope he's wrong.

Time will tell.

Brad Fraser
Toronto
July 23, 2012

Five @ Fifty was first produced by the Royal Exchange Theatre, Manchester, England, on April 12, 2011, with the following cast and crew:

Jan Ravens: Olivia Fairfax
Ingrid Lacey: Tricia Woodcock
Teresa Banham: Norma Goulet
Barbara Barnes: Fern Brown
Candida Gubbins: Lorene Goodman

Director: Braham Murray
Designer: Johanna Bryant
Lighting: Jason Taylor
Sound: John Leonard
Company manager: Lee Drinkwater
Stage manager: Julia Wade
Deputy stage manager: Tracey Fleet
Assistant stage manager: Greg Skipworth

THE CHARACTERS

All aged fifty

Olivia Fairfax
Tricia Woodcock
Norma Goulet
Fern Brown
Lorene Goodman

THE SETTING

Various locations as specified.

PUNCTUATION NOTE

A period is used to indicate the end of vocalization, not necessarily the end of a thought, likewise with capital letters at the beginning of sentences. Commas and other punctuation have been intentionally omitted.

ACT ONE

A doorbell rings. Lights rise on NORMA *and* OLIVIA'S *living room, decorated for a party.*

NORMA   Come in.

TRICIA enters with wine.

TRICIA   Hey.

NORMA   Tissue.

They kiss and hug.

How are you?

TRICIA   Good.

NORMA   You look great. Is that?

TRICIA   Wine. Both colours. As requested.

NORMA   Great. Drink?

TRICIA   I'd blow a monkey for a bourbon.

NORMA   Where did you learn those manners?

TRICIA   Our Lady of Perpetual Sexual Abuse Roman Catholic Elementary School—something's different.

NORMA   I've gained ten pounds.

TRICIA   Oh.

NORMA   I was hoping it was water retention but it's actually just fat thanx for asking.

TRICIA   You should start cooking with a healthy butter alternative.

NORMA   As if.

TRICIA   You know better than butter.

NORMA   Your drink.

TRICIA   Am I early?

NORMA   Always are.

TRICIA   What can I do?

NORMA gives her a hand pump.

NORMA   Tie some balloons while I finish arranging fruit no one will touch.

TRICIA   How are things at the office?

NORMA   Horrifying. This weird viral outbreak has every kid with a cough in the office. And their poor mothers. I don't know how those women cope.

TRICIA   And your own doctor thing?

NORMA   Fine.

TRICIA   What did he say about your blood pressure?

NORMA   High. We might do some drugs to bring it down.

TRICIA   And the sleep thing?

NORMA   Stress. Apnea. I have to go for a sleep test.

TRICIA   I did one of those. It's a nightmare. They stick wires all over your body and your head and then expect you to just go to sleep without sex or drugs or alcohol or anything. How many balloons?

NORMA   Lots. And tie them in pretty bouquets.

TRICIA   Have you told Olivia about it?

NORMA   If it's a problem I'll let her know.

TRICIA   If it's a problem you let me know.

NORMA   Of course. And your leg slash back thing?

TRICIA   Tests and more tests. A touch of arthritis seems likely.

NORMA   Let's hope so.

TRICIA   What else would it be?

NORMA   A blockage or growth.

TRICIA   Very reassuring thanx.

NORMA   Just a possibility. No need to panic.

           The doorbell rings.

           It's open.

           LORENE enters with a gift.

           Early.

LORENE   My last showing was just a couple blocks away.

           NORMA and LORENE kiss. LORENE hands her the gift.

NORMA   Fern's already getting one. We decided.

LORENE   I know but I couldn't just. It's a special day. Hey Tricia.

           They kiss.

TRICIA   I wish you wouldn't do that when we plan a group gift.
           It makes the rest of us look bad.

LORENE   I know but.

NORMA   You're looking good.

LORENE   Really?

NORMA   That's a new dress.

LORENE   It is.

TRICIA   Very fetching. I'm tying balloons into attractive
           bundles.

LORENE   Can I help?

NORMA   Put your gift on the table and get the cheese plate out
           of the fridge. Help yourself to a beer while you're at it.

LORENE   Beer. Yum.

           LORENE exits.

TRICIA   So it's just?

NORMA   The usual suspects yes.

TRICIA   And the birthday babe?

NORMA   Some of those horrible women she works with have taken her for drinks.

TRICIA   I'm so glad Lorene didn't bring the bottom.

NORMA   His name's Clifford.

TRICIA   Clifford's Diana Ross collection makes me very nervous.

NORMA   She swears they have excellent sex.

TRICIA   But what does that mean coming from her?

        LORENE enters with the cheese plate and a beer.

LORENE   I thought Olivia'd want some total blowout for the big five-oh. She's not going to walk in early is she?

TRICIA   She's at a bar. Please.

NORMA   She didn't want a fuss.

LORENE   Damn this is a nice cold beer.

NORMA   I've always loved the unapologetic way you swill it right from the bottle.

LORENE   You'd almost think I was the lesbian.

NORMA   Almost.

LORENE   You and Olivia are so lucky. I envy lesbians but unfor-
             tunately the only thing that can really satisfy me is a
             very large member.

TRICIA   Is Clifford that blessed?

LORENE   He puts the cock in Caucasian.

NORMA   Nice.

LORENE   Ha. Fourth time lucky. But this is the one. I can feel
             it. He's so into me.

             The doorbell rings.

             Fern.

             NORMA opens the door. FERN enters with a gift bag.

FERN   Ladies.

TRICIA   Hey Fern.

             FERN kisses TRICIA.

FERN   Am I late?

NORMA   No you're right on time you just feel late because these
             two always show up early.

FERN kisses LORENE.

LORENE That's a cunning outfit.

FERN Call me a shopaholic.

FERN kisses NORMA.

NORMA You're in amazing shape.

FERN Yoga. My religion. Right after football practice with the boys.

TRICIA How are they?

FERN Giants. And beautiful. You girls won't believe how they've matured.

LORENE White wine?

FERN You're a dear.

TRICIA I haven't seen them for a year.

FERN Nearly two. That's a long time with teenagers. They change so fast.

NORMA Are they doing the girlfriend thing yet?

FERN Miles is. He's been seeing the same girl for nearly a year. She's very nice but Walt and I are trying to break them up. He's young. He shouldn't be getting so attached.

TRICIA   I've always admired your hands-on approach to parenting.

LORENE gives FERN her drink.

FERN   Thank you Lorene. Blake's got a lot of girls calling him but he's fourteen. You know how scared they are at that age. And Donnie's still into comic books and computer games.

FERN notices LORENE's gift.

I thought we agreed on a group gift.

LORENE   I know but it was on sale half price.

NORMA   What is it?

LORENE   Chanel gift set.

TRICIA   What did we get her Fern?

FERN   A pair of diamond earrings. You owe me one thousand dollars each.

Pause.

TRICIA   You're joking.

FERN   Of course I'm joking. Look at the box. It's a set of antique highball glasses. With the ducks painted on them. Like your uncle had behind the bar in his base-ment rec room. You each owe me thirty bucks.

They give money to FERN *as they speak.*

LORENE   I can't believe you got Trish. Diamonds. Hah.

TRICIA   She didn't get me.

LORENE   She totally got you.

FERN   Just because I'm a housewife doesn't mean I don't have a sense of humour.

TRICIA   Normal Ferny's being mean to me.

NORMA   Stand up for yourself.

TRICIA   But she always takes the moral high ground because she has children.

NORMA   You're an award winning newspaper columnist.

TRICIA   But my womb is barren. My ovaries are dusty.

LORENE   Wasn't Dusty Ovaries a country singer?

FERN   I brought a card for everyone to sign.

TRICIA   You think of everything.

FERN   Lorene why don't we put your gift with this one and we'll say we all got her both of them?

LORENE   Because that's my own personal gift.

TRICIA   Great but we'd've all gotten our own personal gift for Olivia if we'd known you were going to do it.

LORENE   I didn't think it would be such a big deal.

FERN   It's not.

TRICIA   But if you agree to something you should do it.

LORENE   Whatever. Jeez.

            FERN sets the card and a pen on the table. The others sign the card as they speak.

NORMA   How's Walt?

FERN   Thankfully not crazy. I talk to a lot of wives our age and their husbands are crazy. Buying sports cars screwing their secretaries getting tattoos you know. How's Clifford?

LORENE   Excellent. He was really pissed when I told him boys weren't allowed tonight.

FERN   Such a lovely guy.

TRICIA   Yes. Lovely.

NORMA   Tricia.

LORENE   Are you being an evil witch?

TRICIA   A bit.

NORMA   We're all evil witches.

TRICIA   From time to time.

LORENE   It's what holds us together.

TRICIA   That and the horrible high school dance where no one actually asked any of us to dance.

NORMA   Let that go.

TRICIA   But it is where we bonded.

LORENE   I never forgot that night.

TRICIA   Is it too early to light a joint?

LORENE   Never.

FERN   Why do you think no one asked us to dance?

LORENE   It's not like we were all unattractive.

TRICIA   We intimidated them.

NORMA   I intimidated them. And I was unattractive.

TRICIA   Maybe it was so we could get to know each other.

TRICIA lights a joint. They all share it.

NORMA   Good one.

LORENE   That smells so great.

FERN   I shouldn't but I will.

TRICIA   You always say that.

FERN   I only smoke when I'm with you guys. Last time I came home and ate half a pan of date squares and laughed hysterically at everything Walt said to me. If he'd noticed—

NORMA   Pass it on.

FERN   He's very "anti drugs."

LORENE   No one can see us from the street can they?

NORMA   It's fine. Relax.

LORENE   I do have a professional reputation to maintain.

FERN   Is that cheese?

NORMA   There's sour cream dip as well.

LORENE   And stuffed artichokes—and plump little dumplings— aren't they darling.

NORMA   And gravy for dipping.

TRICIA   No point coming to Norma and Olivia's if you're not
            gonna pig out.

NORMA   I enjoy cooking.

LORENE   Who needs a fresh up?

NORMA   Let me.

LORENE   I can do it.

            LORENE exits to the kitchen.

FERN   Do you think she knows Clifford is gay?

TRICIA   No.

FERN   Oh dear.

NORMA   As long as they're happy.

FERN   Are you seeing anyone Trish?

TRICIA   Not at the moment.

FERN   What happened to that nice man from India?

TRICIA   He neglected to inform me he was married in India.

NORMA   Oh no.

TRICIA   Oh yeah. Six months of seeing one another and two weeks ago his heretofore unknown to me heartbreakingly handsome son shows up while Mister India's in the shower and I'm making breakfast.

FERN   Seriously?

TRICIA   It was all very civilized. Apparently I wasn't the first concubine Interjit had taken up with in North America. I don't mind being someone's mistress if I know I'm their mistress but when they lie to me—

FERN   Those people are accustomed to multiple partners. Deception is easy for them. Like Mormons.

NORMA   Fern.

TRICIA   Where's that joint?

NORMA   Over here.

LORENE enters with drinks.

LORENE   Freshies for everyone.

TRICIA   You're so handy.

LORENE   Never having been pretty enough to whore my way to the top I learned to mix and carry drinks at an early age.

TRICIA   Not as hard on your knees.

FERN   Stop.

TRICIA   Remember when oral sex was taboo?

LORENE   Do I? That was my special thing. Oral. Every Jewish girl
            has a special thing. Like some sewed or embroidered
            or sang or played the piano. Then one day it was like
            everyone was playing the fucking piano.

FERN   Lorene.

LORENE   I had to resort to taking it in the butt just to keep them
            interested.

FERN   Lorene!

LORENE   Ha!

FERN   I still prefer sex to be paired with romance.

LORENE   Yeah but you've been married to the same dude since
            you were twenty-one—you have no conception of how
            the real world works—

            OLIVIA *enters suddenly and screams.*

OLIVIA   Surprise!

TRICIA   Fuck!

NORMA   Jesus!

FERN   Olivia!

NORMA   You were supposed to call before you left the bar.

OLIVIA   I knew you girls'd be waiting for me. Air kisses for everyone.

FERN   You knew?

OLIVIA   Kinda not hard to put it together.

TRICIA   You didn't drive.

OLIVIA   I haven't had that much to drink.

> *OLIVIA **kisses** NORMA.*

NORMA   Welcome home.

OLIVIA   Is that pot I smell?

TRICIA   I've got more.

OLIVIA   Spark it up. Who's mixing the drinks?

LORENE   What's your poison?

OLIVIA   Vodka. Rocks. Why isn't there any music?

NORMA   We like to talk.

OLIVIA   It's a party. I want music.

NORMA   It's so distracting.

OLIVIA   We are old aren't we?

TRICIA   Fifty.

OLIVIA   Jesus. How did that happen?

FERN   It sneaks up on you.

TRICIA   That's right. You turned fifty already.

FERN   Last February.

LORENE   You were supposed to remind us.

FERN   I spent it with my family.

NORMA   So tonight's a double celebration.

OLIVIA   Oh sure. Make me share my birthday with the beautiful one.

FERN   Tonight should be all about you.

OLIVIA   I know.

FERN   I have other people who love me.

LORENE   Ha.

FERN   You know what I mean.

NORMA   I made dumplings.

OLIVIA   Joint?

TRICIA   Right here.

NORMA   My mother was old when she was fifty.

OLIVIA   I don't feel a day over forty-two.

NORMA   And you don't look a day over thirty-five.

LORENE   If you're squinting through a dirty fish tank.

OLIVIA   At midnight!

LORENE   Ha!

OLIVIA   To fucking fifty.

              All raise their glasses in a toast.

ALL   To fucking fifty!

              TRICIA *raises her glass again.*

TRICIA   And the fact that unlike a lot of other people we know
             none of us has cancer.

OLIVIA   No sick friends on my birthday. It's sad but boring.

NORMA   Eat.

LORENE   Drink. Who needs more?

TRICIA   No one's driving right?

FERN   Walt's on standby.

LORENE   Clifford will come whenever I call.

TRICIA   I'll walk.

LORENE   It's not safe the way you roam the streets at night.

TRICIA   I can take care of myself.

NORMA   She can. I've seen her.

OLIVIA   Tricia can do anything.

TRICIA   I suck at sports.

FERN   I loved that piece you did on the way the river parks have degenerated.

TRICIA   People keep dumping and the city does nothing.

LORENE   The one about putting Bogie down was wonderful too. Dead pets always make me cry.

TRICIA   The hardest thing I've ever written.

OLIVIA   Quit talking about her. It's my birthday.

FERN   How does if feel?

OLIVIA   It's wonderful.

FERN   Your life is blessed.

TRICIA   Who woulda thought after meeting in grade eleven you two would still be together?

LORENE   Your relationship's lasted longer than anyone's—even Fern's.

TRICIA   Which is pretty wild considering you didn't even admit you were lovers until you were thirty.

NORMA   Tricia.

OLIVIA   She wanted to but I never would until she told me she'd leave if I didn't put out.

NORMA   Livy—

OLIVIA   I loved her so what could I do?

FERN   Is that true?

NORMA   She's had a bit to drink.

OLIVIA   There were plenty of men who wanted me but no one ever loved me as much as Norma did.

TRICIA   And all that time I was sure you were both licking each
           other the second we left the room.

OLIVIA   Nope. We played around a bit but just best friend stuff.
           I was scared.

TRICIA   Scared?

FERN   I know what you mean.

NORMA   Luckily she came around.

OLIVIA   At thirtysomething.

LORENE   You waited fifteen years to have sex with her?

FERN   That's devotion.

TRICIA   That's pathetic.

LORENE   So you're not a real lesbian?

OLIVIA   I am the person who loves Norma. And we have some
           amazing sex so shut up. We went to Jackson's Cape for
           dinner the other night. It was so good. The music was
           a bit loud but the room was really nice and the food.
           We started with scallops wrapped in bacon a shrimp
           remoulade and a gumbo for the table.

LORENE   There were other people at the table?

OLIVIA   No. Norma was going to have the lamb but I wanted
          the lamb so I talked her into trying the catfish with
          the shrimp étouffée and we got the buckwheat pasta
          with chorizo for the table.

TRICIA   That's one well fed table.

OLIVIA   They had seven different dessert choices. Lemon
          cream apple crumble dulce de leche torte—

TRICIA   We're getting all the dessert choices too?

OLIVIA   Watermelon ice cream sticky butterscotch pudding.

NORMA   Gâteau Saint-Honoré.

OLIVIA   And one more.

TRICIA   It doesn't really matter.

OLIVIA   Sssh. What was it?

NORMA   I can't.

OLIVIA   Lemon cream apple crumble dulce de leche torte
          watermelon ice cream sticky butterscotch pudding
          gâteau Saint-Honoré and.

NORMA   Figs.

OLIVIA   Stone warmed figs in maple syrup and crème fraîche?

NORMA   No that was at the Diplomatico.

OLIVIA   Then what?

NORMA   I can't.

OLIVIA   Lemon cream apple crumble.

TRICIA   Really?

OLIVIA   Hush. Dulce de leche torte watermelon ice cream.

FERN   Livy.

OLIVIA   Sticky butterscotch pudding gâteau Saint-Honoré and.

NORMA
& OLIVIA   TIRAMISU.

LORENE   Thank god.

OLIVIA   Norma had the gâteau. I had the crumble.

TRICIA   Fascinating.

OLIVIA   Don't be so sour.

FERN   It sounds very good.

NORMA   Time for cake.

LORENE   Y'think?

NORMA exits.

OLIVIA   Why is my glass empty?

FERN   Let me refill it.

OLIVIA   Thank you Fern. Everyone refill your glasses. We're going to sing old show tunes. Really loud.

TRICIA   No.

NORMA enters with a cake lit by a single candle and leads them in a brisk version of "Happy Birthday."

LORENE   Now make a wish and blow out the candle.

OLIVIA   I'm wishing for smooth skin and firmer boobs.

TRICIA   Throw in a waist.

OLIVIA   Cow.

FERN   Blow.

OLIVIA blows out the candle. Everyone claps. NORMA cuts and serves the cake.

TRICIA   Tiny pieces for the dieters.

OLIVIA   And big ones for the hogs.

FERN   Omigod look!

NORMA   Double creamy chocolate ganache.

LORENE   I just peed a little bit when you said that.

NORMA   And there's fake whipped cream made from an edible oil product to squirt on top.

FERN   You're evil.

NORMA   Just to take the edge off.

LORENE   This is so good.

TRICIA   But so bad.

NORMA   Almost forgot.

>   NORMA *exits to the kitchen.*

FERN   Forgot what?

OLIVIA   Our special treat.

LORENE   Is it something else to eat?

TRICIA   That would just be mean.

>   NORMA *enters with champagne.*

NORMA   Ta da!

The other women clap and squeal with pleasure as NOR-MA opens the bottle.

FERN   Ooh champagne.

TRICIA   The expensive stuff. I love it.

NORMA   Everyone grab a glass.

The champagne is poured.

FERN   Yum.

LORENE   Speech from the birthday girl. Speech speech.

OLIVIA   Oh stop.

NORMA   Speech.

OLIVIA   Okay. Thank you all. My bestest friends. So nice of you to come and give me gifts. And cake. Champagne. I'm fat. But I'm happy. And I know you all look down on me. I'm kidding. You don't look down on me. I look down on you. All of you. Especially Tricia. Kidding. Tricia's the best. Of all of us. She can do anything.

TRICIA   Okay—

OLIVIA   And Fern who's still got the same husband. And Lorene who married—all those guys. And Tricia with all of her meaningless sexual encounters and—

TRICIA   God bless us every one.

ALL BUT
OLIVIA &
TRICIA   GOD BLESS US EVERY ONE.

OLIVIA   I wasn't done.

LORENE   We got the gist.

NORMA   Have more cake.

OLIVIA   I don't want any fucking cake where are my presents?

FERN   Here. This is from all of us.

LORENE   Except me. I got you my own gift.

TRICIA   Lorene.

LORENE   What? I did.

    OLIVIA shakes the package.

OLIVIA   Oh this feels really like—

FERN   Careful.

    OLIVIA drops the package. Sound of glasses shattering.
    Pause.

OLIVIA   Glasses.

FERN   Duck glasses.

OLIVIA   I love them.

TRICIA   You broke them.

OLIVIA   They slipped.

NORMA   It's alright. They broke in the box. No damage done.

TRICIA   If you don't count the smashed antique glasses.

OLIVIA   They were antique? I have the best friends.

LORENE   Now aren't we glad there's a second gift? Here. Try not
              to drop it.

TRICIA   Handy.

LORENE   Yeah.

OLIVIA   Chanel I love it wow great thanx a lot.

LORENE   Really?

OLIVIA   Totally mean it where's my drink?

NORMA   Right here.

OLIVIA   That's it for fucking presents? Some broken duck
              glasses and a Chanel gift set?

NORMA   I got you something.

OLIVIA   Goody.

FERN   What is it?

> NORMA *produces a ring box and hands it to* OLIVIA.

NORMA   For your fiftieth.

OLIVIA   It's a ring.

TRICIA   Y'think?

> OLIVIA *opens the box.*

FERN   Are we witnessing a proposal?

> *Pause.*

NORMA   It's just a friendship ring.

TRICIA   Oh please.

OLIVIA   Thank you.

> OLIVIA *and* NORMA *kiss.*

FERN   Aw.

NORMA   You're welcome.

OLIVIA   I love you.

LORENE   Get a room.

OLIVIA   I love you all where's the champagne?

TRICIA   You just refilled your glass.

OLIVIA   Who's all of a sudden the drink police?

TRICIA   I'm just.

OLIVIA   Mind your business.

FERN   I'm gonna contact Walter.

TRICIA   Right.

OLIVIA   More drinks.

FERN   Oh I think I've had enough.

OLIVIA   But it's my birthday.

FERN   I have to be up early.

OLIVIA pours champagne into FERN's glass.

OLIVIA   Drink.

FERN   I don't.

OLIVIA   Drink.

TRICIA   Stop bullying her.

OLIVIA   It's my fucking birthday. We're all supposed to get drunk.

FERN   I'm drunk enough.

LORENE   Me too.

NORMA   Why don't I make some coffee?

OLIVIA   Jesus Christ you're all so fucking boring.

LORENE   Olivia.

> OLIVIA *suddenly pukes all over* TRICIA. *Long pause.*

TRICIA   Back to charm school.

LORENE   Olivia.

FERN   Eeew.

NORMA   I'll get a washcloth.

> NORMA *exits.*

FERN   Are you alright?

OLIVIA   Fine.

FERN   I meant Tricia.

TRICIA   Fine except for the puke.

FERN .   Good.

LORENE   Oy.

OLIVIA   Sorry sorry happy boiday.

FERN   Olivia.

OLIVIA   Tired now. Sorry.

            OLIVIA exits.

LORENE   Happy birthday.

            *NORMA enters with a washcloth. She wipes the puke
            off of TRICIA.*

NORMA   I don't know if she ate any dinner.

TRICIA   It smells like lunch.

            A car horn is heard off.

FERN   That'll be Walter.

NORMA   Perfect timing.

FERN   Lorene we go right past your place.

LORENE   You don't mind? It would save calling Clifford.

FERN   Of course not.

LORENE   Thank you.

FERN   Tricia?

TRICIA   I'll help Norma clean up.

LORENE   You sure?

TRICIA   I'll be fine.

FERN   Good night. Merci.

NORMA   Night.

LORENE   Lovely party.

> LORENE *and* FERN *exit.* NORMA *and* TRICIA *tidy up
> without saying anything for a moment.*

TRICIA   That was a proposal.

NORMA   Tricia I've been living with Olivia for over twenty years.
             I don't need a wedding to make it official.

TRICIA   That doesn't mean you wouldn't like one.

NORMA   Let it go.

TRICIA   Will you be able to sleep?

NORMA   As much as I ever do.

TRICIA   Joint?

NORMA   It's too late.

TRICIA   About this puking thing—

NORMA   It's her birthday. She got a little emotional and out
           of control. Don't make a drama out of it please Trish.
           Tomorrow she'll feel so bad.

           Short pause.

TRICIA   Okay. I'm off.

NORMA   Thanx.

           They embrace and kiss. A light rises on LORENE alone.

LORENE   Shalimar. A dab on the underside of each wrist—behind
           each ear. It hung around after she left—sometimes
           for days—almost like she was still there but invis-
           ible. When she first got sick and I sat with her in that
           place—she was unconscious—I put my hand around
           her wrist and held it just for a few minutes and I could
           smell Shalimar on my fingertips for months afterward.
           It clung to me like—guilt for not being a better daugh-
           ter—not being a better mother. Shalimar. The smell
           of someone who's never really been there.

A light on FERN; *she's in her living room on her yoga mat.*

FERN   Stretch and breathe. Breathe. Breathe.

TRICIA enters.

TRICIA   Hey stranger. So glad you called.

FERN   You're early.

TRICIA   I am?

FERN   Twenty minutes.

TRICIA   We can chat while you stretch.

FERN   Don't be silly. I can—

TRICIA   Seriously. Shut up and yoga.

FERN performs yoga as they speak.

FERN   It's a beautiful day.

TRICIA   Where are the boys?

FERN   They're never home in the summer. All of our meaning-ful contact comes through electronic communication devices. Do you want to join me?

TRICIA   What?

FERN   Stretch with me. It's wonderful. You won't be able to stop.

TRICIA   Thanx but I've got some naggy back thing going on. Who's that guy?

FERN   Where?

TRICIA   Across the street. Beige house.

FERN   Oh Barry. His wife's Linda the rusty haired IT developer.

TRICIA   They come to all your seasonal blah blahs.

FERN   For nearly twenty years.

TRICIA   He's a—?

FERN   Graphic artist. Works out of his home. A boy and a girl. Both in university.

TRICIA   Designer.

FERN   Pardon?

TRICIA   They call them graphic designers now because they work on computers.

FERN   Right.

TRICIA   Nice legs.

FERN   He's a nice guy.

TRICIA   Aw now he's going into the house. Bye Barry.

FERN   I have iced tea filtered water or pomegranate juice.

TRICIA   How about a diet whatever? I'm hooked on the
            aspartame.

> *FERN's finished. She towels off, rolls up her mat, etc. as
> they speak.*

FERN   No.

TRICIA   Coffee?

FERN   Can't live without it. Fresh in the maker.

> *FERN gets coffee.*

TRICIA   Do you have a cleaning lady?

FERN   Shiera from Trinidad. I'd be lost without her.

TRICIA   I need a Shiera from Trinidad. It takes forever to clean
            my place.

> *FERN gets herself a cup of coffee.*

FERN   Do you think that was a proposal the other night?

TRICIA   I think it's as close as Norma will ever get.

FERN   I felt a bit bad for her.

TRICIA   They've been together long enough for her to know
            how it works.

FERN   You'd hope. How long has Olivia been getting drunk
            like that?

TRICIA   I'm not sure.

FERN   She used to be so much fun.

TRICIA   If high maintenance.

FERN   She told such wonderful stories.

TRICIA   Yeah.

FERN   But now it's just all those lists. What she ate. Those
            people she works with. What they watched on TV. She
            doesn't look well either.

TRICIA   How could she? They live on meat lard gravy and cake.

FERN   How much is she drinking?

TRICIA   Almost constantly.

FERN   Why haven't you said something?

TRICIA   I have. A couple times. In that sort of are you sure you should be doing that kind of way. She just laughs and tells me there's nothing to worry about.

FERN   I was sure she was drunk at Donnie's junior grad.

TRICIA   Shit.

FERN   What?

TRICIA   She's an alcoholic isn't she?

FERN   I think so.

TRICIA   Goddamn it.

FERN   Do you think someone should talk to her?

TRICIA   Yes. But who?

FERN   Whoever's closest to her.

TRICIA   Lorene.

FERN   Absolutely.

A light rises on LORENE *in her kitchen with a cup of coffee.*

LORENE   Me? Why me?

FERN and TRICIA *join her with coffee cups.*

TRICIA   You've known her the longest.

FERN   She listens to you more than she listens to anyone else.

LORENE   Tricia usually does the hard stuff.

TRICIA   But she relates to you best.

LORENE   Yeah but.

FERN   We have to say something.

LORENE   Really?

TRICIA   Lorene.

Pause.

LORENE   I'll talk to Olivia if you'll talk to Norma.

FERN   She's her enabler.

TRICIA   Maybe we should consult a professional first.

LORENE   Professional what?

TRICIA   Addictions counsellor psychotherapist witch doctor you know.

FERN   Don't you think if any of us were dealing with this we'd appreciate having it kept in the family for as long as possible?

TRICIA   We're just gonna talk to her.

LORENE   Do you think it's because she doesn't want to be a les-
             bian anymore?

FERN   Was she ever a lesbian to begin with?

LORENE   Is this any of our business — really?

TRICIA   You don't think there's a problem?

LORENE   Lotsa people drink a lot. Including us.

FERN   But not every day.

TRICIA   All day long. With wild mood swings. It's all classic
             shit.

LORENE   You know how mad she gets.

FERN   I think the trick is to speak to both of them gently.
             Out of a caring place.

TRICIA   Identify the problem and deal with it.

LORENE   I guess that's what real friends do.

TRICIA   Exactly.

             A light on NORMA *alone in her office filling out medi-
             cal forms.*

NORMA We were watching the Big Monkey Movie—it was actually the Big Money Movie but that's what we called it—on that new cablevision station in her basement rec room. It was some black and white British monstrosity called *Island of Terror* about these bone sucking turtle monsters that was actually scarier than it sounds and we just kept moving closer and closer together under the quilt until my hand was on her thigh and she didn't move away. She didn't respond but she didn't move away. We kept watching the movie but our breathing had changed. I thought she could hear my heart beating. I started to say something but she just shook her head without looking away from the TV. Then she let me keep my hand there for the rest of the movie. It was so painful. So perfect. So much more than I ever hoped for.

Lights rise on OLIVIA *at a table in a restaurant. She's drinking a glass of white wine. There is a fresh beer on the table.* LORENE *enters.*

LORENE Sorry traffic's a bitch.

OLIVIA Don't worry. I just got here two wines ago myself. You look great in that.

LORENE Thanx. You too.

OLIVIA I like this place. It's got a vibe. I ordered you a beer.

LORENE Thanx.

OLIVIA   Check out our waiter.

LORENE   Where?

OLIVIA   The brunette with the big shoulders and bad haircut.

LORENE   Nothing wrong with that.

OLIVIA   Very nice butt.

LORENE   Indeed. You ever miss it?

OLIVIA   Miss what?

LORENE   The dick.

OLIVIA   They have the best barbecued pork ribs here. The best.
            The best.

LORENE   How's work?

OLIVIA   Marlene's sister's daughter finally gave her the baby so
            she could move in with her boyfriend.

LORENE   Really?

OLIVIA   She's the document master remember?

LORENE   Right.

OLIVIA   Her niece is the abusive mother with the Swiss
            boyfriend.

LORENE   Sure.

OLIVIA   And Mandy's husband Milt had a cancerous testicle removed. You know they do it through a small incision in the abdomen. I thought they'd have to cut the sack open completely but disappointingly no. Robert's mother went into the hospital with a tumour on her tongue and they cut one whole side of it off. And a big chunk of her jaw and a bit of her neck. Martin had some bathroom event that got him into trouble. I asked around but no one knows the details.

LORENE   You're okay though?

OLIVIA   Oh please I've got so much seniority I'd have to kill someone more important than my supervisor in a very nasty manner to be dismissed. Another five years and I retire with a full pension.

LORENE   Enjoy it. Not many get to retire like that anymore.

OLIVIA   I know. Full health and dental plus eighty percent of my final salary for life—amazing death benefits. Mahogany casket. Headstone with a statue of Jesus or Mohamed or Satan or whoever you're into.

LORENE   Lucky.

OLIVIA   Selling any houses?

LORENE   Omigod it's like stealing from people. The market's so hot right now. And the interest rates.

OLIVIA   We haven't had lunch in like forever.

LORENE   We get so busy.

OLIVIA   Tell me about it. But it has to stop. We go back the
           farthest of all of us.

LORENE   We do. That is a beautiful ring.

OLIVIA   Isn't it?

LORENE   Stunning.

           Pause.

OLIVIA   What?

LORENE   I just nothing actually but Tricia thought I should talk
           to you.

OLIVIA   Tricia?

LORENE   Yeah.

OLIVIA   Are you okay?

LORENE   What? Yeah.

OLIVIA   It's just—

LORENE   Yeah?

OLIVIA   You've been—

LORENE   What?

OLIVIA   How's Clifford?

LORENE   Great.

OLIVIA   You guys are fine?

LORENE   Stronger than ever.

OLIVIA   I've been—concerned.

LORENE   Why?

OLIVIA   I guess I just—I want to know that you're alright—that you're getting what you need.

LORENE   Why wouldn't I be?

OLIVIA   I don't know. Aren't you?

LORENE   Sure yeah what?

OLIVIA   I just want to make sure you're okay.

LORENE   Don't I seem okay?

OLIVIA   I can tell when something's bothering you.

LORENE   Nothing's bothering me.

OLIVIA   Not even the children?

LORENE   Why are you bringing them up?

OLIVIA   You started this conversation.

LORENE   No.

OLIVIA   You did.

LORENE   I just meant to—

OLIVIA   What?

LORENE   Where's the fucking waiter?

OLIVIA   Something's bothering you.

LORENE   I felt their fathers were more suitable parents than me—you know that.

OLIVIA   You're upset.

LORENE   No where's that waiter I need another beer.

OLIVIA   I could use a fresh one too. Was there something specific you wanted to talk to me about?

LORENE   No—nothing no.

> *Lights rise on* TRICIA *and* NORMA *sharing a joint and playing cribbage.*

TRICIA   Fifteen two fifteen four fifteen six fifteen eight and a pair is ten and a double run is sixteen.

NORMA   Ignorant whore.

TRICIA   You dealt.

NORMA   You want a diet whatever?

TRICIA   Of course. I'm so glad your work hours end nice and early.

NORMA   Finish this. Maybe not much longer.

TRICIA   Why not?

NORMA hands the joint to TRICIA and exits to the kitchen but speaks off.

NORMA   They're pushing me to take more patients. Did you know for every kid that moves on to a GP there are two more waiting to take its place?

TRICIA   Has it gotten so bad?

NORMA   They really only want us to drug them anyway. What are you working on?

NORMA enters with drinks and snacks.

TRICIA   Something refuting the whole sexuality has no choice paradigm—that all people are born gay or straight shit.

NORMA   That'll make you popular. Eat. The pork things rock.

TRICIA   Internet porn has made a lot of unimaginative people
            realize there are a lot more choices than they were
            aware of.

NORMA   Everything's so accessible. Ten years ago if these kids
            knew some of that stuff they know now it would've
            been a sure sign of sexual abuse. Now it just means
            they know how to work a mouse.

TRICIA   When we were girls seeing a man's dick in a movie or
            magazine was like totally verboten.

NORMA   Just didn't happen.

TRICIA   But now.

NORMA   Penis is the new tits.

TRICIA   Exactly.

NORMA   Dating anyone new?

TRICIA   Need a break.

NORMA   You'll meet someone. You always do.

TRICIA   I'm not really that concerned.

NORMA   Seriously?

TRICIA   It's like the older I've gotten the less it's mattered. I
         mean it'd be great to meet someone I adore but all the
         shit that comes with a relationship—not so much.

NORMA   I don't think I could handle being on my own.

TRICIA   Don't sell yourself short.

NORMA   Olivia's enough for me.

         NORMA shuffles the cards.

TRICIA   Speaking of.

NORMA   Yeah?

TRICIA   Olivia's drinking slash puking thing.

NORMA   Tricia.

TRICIA   She has a problem Norma.

NORMA   What can I do besides express my concern?

TRICIA   Ask her to stop.

NORMA   Do you think I haven't?

TRICIA   Why can't she just get pissed like everyone else? Why
         does it always get stupid or ugly? I don't get it.

         NORMA deals.

NORMA   She hardly ever does anything embarrassing.

TRICIA   She did barf on me.

NORMA   It's not like you never barfed on her.

TRICIA   That was thirty-two years ago with four people crammed into the back seat of a Honda Civic while drinking lemon gin. It's not even remotely the same thing.

NORMA   We are middle-aged people. We need to be tolerant of one another.

TRICIA   Not if it makes things worse.

NORMA   I'll let you know when it's a problem.

TRICIA   You don't think her behaviour at the party was a problem?

NORMA   No. And that's my opinion as a doctor and her partner.

TRICIA   Normal—

NORMA   Stop.

        Pause.

TRICIA   Deal.

        NORMA *deals the cards. They discard to the crib and play.*

Two.

NORMA   Pair for four.

TRICIA   Triple pair for six.

NORMA   Nine for fifteen.

TRICIA   Nine for twenty-four.

NORMA   Three for twenty-seven.

TRICIA   Three more for thirty two for a pair and a go for one.

NORMA   You are the devil.

TRICIA   I am.

Lights rise on FERN *alone, stretching.*

FERN   He's solid. Reliable. The perfect husband and father.
               A very nice body even if he is a bit short. I wanted his
               children. I wanted his sperm inside of me. I just did.
               From the second I saw him. I'd never—it was like I
               had no choice. So I married him and I thought I was
               the luckiest young woman in the whole wide world. I
               was going to have his babies and that was exactly what
               I wanted.

               LORENE enters.

LORENE   Is that all you do?

FERN   Staying fit is the best way to battle things like depression and bone loss.

LORENE   Menopause. Oy.

FERN   I can't stand the hot flashes and the dry eyes.

                LORENE opens the fridge and gets herself some water.

LORENE   I can't stand that I've been having my period for the last three months.

FERN   Eew.

LORENE   Just a slight but constant ooze.

FERN   I'm intermittent and spotty.

LORENE   Did you go through that phase where anything touching your vagina was painful?

FERN   No. Just a bit dry. How did the lunch with Olivia go?

LORENE   Okay.

FERN   Did you talk about her drinking?

LORENE   No.

FERN   Tissue's gonna be pissed.

LORENE   Tissue isn't the boss of me.

FERN   But you said.

LORENE   Shit happens. Anyway it could be just a power thing.
              You know how she and Olivia are.

FERN   They've always been at each other.

LORENE   It's because Trish and Norma get on so well.

FERN   I always thought they were more compatible.

LORENE   I know. But you know how straight Tricia is.

FERN   I don't think she's into fat people either.

LORENE   Olivia's always resented her.

FERN   Ever since the Ophelia event.

LORENE   Yes.

              *TRICIA enters. She goes to the fridge and looks for a diet
              cola.*

TRICIA   You're not really speculating that my concern for Olivia
              comes from the fact that she still thinks I stole the
              part of Ophelia from her in our high school produc-
              tion of *Hamlet* are you?

LORENE   You're a witch.

FERN   It's her bionic hearing.

TRICIA   You chickened out on talking to her.

LORENE   I got—sidetracked.

TRICIA   Oh for.

LORENE   She brought up my kids.

             Pause.

TRICIA   That's unfair.

LORENE   Is it? Those kids are personal territory for me. A private thing. That's what she was telling me about her drinking. It's a private thing. If I want to talk about her private thing she gets to talk about my private thing. Isn't that how it works?

TRICIA   Not if your private thing is killing you.

LORENE   I'm not really prepared to get all confrontational over this.

FERN   What did Norma say?

TRICIA   Mind your own business.

LORENE   See.

TRICIA   So we just stand by and watch her drink herself to death?

LORENE   It's what our mothers did for our fathers.

FERN   My father rarely drank. Why is she an alcoholic anyway?

LORENE   I never knew her mother to drink.

TRICIA   That woman barely left the house.

LORENE   And the father died so young.

FERN   Maybe witnessing the accident did it to her.

TRICIA   We've all got childhood traumas.

LORENE   Not as good as yours.

FERN   Really.

LORENE   All of those mining towns and trailer parks.

FERN   And those creepy drunken relatives.

TRICIA   And while my Dickensian childhood may make me severely screwed up I am not a drunk. Although I should be. Also a heroin addict and a serial killer. But I am not.

LORENE   There's no way we can win at this.

TRICIA   She's our friend.

LORENE   It's too bloody hard.

TRICIA   So that's it?

LORENE   Yeah.

    LORENE exits.

FERN   What more can we do?

    FERN exits.

TRICIA   Shit.

    Lights rise on OLIVIA checking the place settings on a large restaurant table as she speaks.

OLIVIA   I remember my mother holding me on the edge of this wide empty—airfield I guess—and this strong hot wind from the helicopter. It took my breath away. I like to think there were visible forest fires on the hills around us but that might just be adding detail from what I learned later. I do remember the smell of smoke. There's a man waving to me from the helicopter only he's wearing a flight suit and a helmet with a mask so I can't see his face but he's completely my father. I can tell from the way he's standing and waving. Then the helicopter's taking off and everyone's clapping and there's this poof sound—not very loud—and an orange ball in the air where the helicopter was. That's my dad. The hero in the orange ball of flame that goes poof over the airfield on its way to rescue some people from a forest fire. Orange ball. Poof. Bye.

*TRICIA **enters.***

TRICIA   Hi.

OLIVIA   Early.

TRICIA   Where's Norma?

OLIVIA   There was some thing at the office so she's gonna be late.

TRICIA   Place cards?

OLIVIA   It's a special occasion.

TRICIA   Does it really matter where we sit?

OLIVIA   It matters to me.

TRICIA   Nice wines.

OLIVIA   Yes.

TRICIA   May I?

OLIVIA   Go ahead. I told the waiter to hold on cocktail orders until everyone arrives.

TRICIA   Great spread.

OLIVIA   These are just the starters. Wait until you see what the
           dinner choices are. Braised beef ribs—

TRICIA   How 'bout we let the menu be a lovely surprise. Did
           you hear my column about the Rochester's illegal de-
           mise has been nominated for a Bakely?

OLIVIA   A what?

TRICIA   This national press award.

OLIVIA   Nice do you like the centrepiece?

TRICIA   Beautiful. You're looking good.

OLIVIA   New hair style.

TRICIA   Brightens you up quite nicely.

OLIVIA   The dress is new too.

TRICIA   I can tell. Have you been drinking?

OLIVIA   I have a dinner to pull together.

TRICIA   Good for you.

OLIVIA   I'm not hopeless Trish.

TRICIA   Things are alright?

OLIVIA   Of course.

TRICIA   No pressure at work? Nothing bad happening at home?

OLIVIA   Are you like trying to talk to me about my drinking?

TRICIA   Yes.

OLIVIA   It's not a problem.

TRICIA   You puked on me.

OLIVIA   And you puked on me.

TRICIA   Don't you people ever let anything go?

OLIVIA   And it just happened to be the night *Hamlet* closed.

TRICIA   We were coming home from the cast party. Everyone was blitzed.

OLIVIA   After your triumphant performance.

TRICIA   I did not steal Ophelia from you. We both read for it and Mr. Dockins thought I read better.

OLIVIA   You got all the leads. Laura in *Glass Menagerie* the mother in *Man-in-the-Moon Marigolds* Tevye in *Fiddler on the Roof*.

TRICIA   It's not my fault none of the boys could sing low enough.

OLIVIA   Just let me play Ophelia I asked. It's my favourite play.
         My favourite part. All you had to do was you know
         tone your reading down a bit. Be a little less—good—
         for a change.

TRICIA   You always do this.

OLIVIA   What?

TRICIA   Start in on all this old shit that doesn't matter any more
         until I have no choice but to.

OLIVIA   What?

TRICIA   Nothing.

OLIVIA   Tell me.

TRICIA   Let it go.

OLIVIA   You do love to make it all about you.

TRICIA   What are you talking about? I didn't—

OLIVIA   Little miss me me me me me.

TRICIA   I did tone my reading down.

                   Pause.

OLIVIA   Liar.

TRICIA   Whatever.

OLIVIA   More wine?

TRICIA   Thanx.

> OLIVIA *refills* TRICIA'S *glass and then pours herself a glass as well.*

I thought you weren't drinking.

OLIVIA   What happened to Cameljack?

TRICIA   Interjit.

OLIVIA   Whatever.

TRICIA   He was married.

OLIVIA   Are you okay?

TRICIA   I'm fine.

OLIVIA   Because you seem very uptight lately.

TRICIA   Do I?

OLIVIA   You've gotten very intense and it's giving you that line between your eyebrows. Do you have a lover of some sort? I know how you get when you're not having regular sex.

TRICIA   Olivia.

OLIVIA   You're not still hanging out at bars until all hours and
            going home with anyone who asks are you?

TRICIA   No.

OLIVIA   What about the computer?

TRICIA   Shut up.

OLIVIA   Whatever happens you know you'll always have us.

TRICIA   Right.

            FERN enters with a gift. OLIVIA *drinks throughout.*

FERN   Hi.

OLIVIA   Thanx for coming.

            FERN and OLIVIA *hug and kiss.*

TRICIA   Wine?

FERN   White. Where should I put this?

TRICIA   On the table with the ice bucket. What is it?

FERN   Hammer Horror the Ingrid Pitt years.

OLIVIA   She'll love them.

TRICIA   Her Ingrid Pitt thing.

OLIVIA   Horror movies brought us together.

                  TRICIA gives FERN wine. They kiss.

FERN   Ooh place cards.

TRICIA   All the best cotillions have them.

OLIVIA   Where's the open bottle?

TRICIA   Right here.

FERN   Did I miss anything?

OLIVIA   Tricia was just talking about what a bad actor I was.

TRICIA   I said no such thing.

OLIVIA   Yes you—

FERN   Let it go.

TRICIA   Exactly. There's no winning.

OLIVIA   How are my boys?

TRICIA   Did you manage to ruin Miles's budding relationship with the girl you disapproved of?

FERN   No. It's a bit worrisome.

TRICIA   They all stand up for themselves eventually.

OLIVIA   Not if you have a wonderful mother like I did. She did everything for me until the day I moved out.

TRICIA   At thirty.

NORMA enters.

NORMA   Late. Sorry. Office complication. Oh look wine don't mind if I do.

FERN   Let me pour.

TRICIA   Happy boiday!

A quick hug and kiss.

OLIVIA   Isn't this private dining room lovely?

NORMA   Exquisite.

NORMA and OLIVIA kiss quickly.

FERN   Wine.

NORMA and FERN embrace and kiss.

NORMA   Where's Lorene?

TRICIA   She usually arrives moments after I do.

NORMA   We haven't heard much from her lately.

FERN   Neither have I.

OLIVIA   Which is not usually a great sign.

NORMA   Congrats on the Bakely nomination by the way.

TRICIA   Thank you.

NORMA   That'll teach evil corporations to tear down historical landmarks illegally.

FERN   I read about it on the computer this morning.

NORMA   How's Walt?

FERN   Great. Sends his best.

OLIVIA   Why don't we all sit in our places now?

TRICIA   Why don't we wait until Lorene arrives?

OLIVIA   But I'd like to see everyone in their places the way I arranged it.

TRICIA   Relax.

OLIVIA   I personally sampled everything we're going to have tonight. It will be spectacular. Braised.

FERN   I'm considering a facelift.

OLIVIA   What?

NORMA   You're the last one who needs a lift.

FERN   Not right this moment. Eventually.

TRICIA   I have to admit I wouldn't mind having something
            done to my boobs. They're a bit.

OLIVIA   Yeah.

TRICIA `   Hey.

OLIVIA   And the eye bags.

TRICIA   I earned these eye bags honestly.

FERN   I say nothing before fifty-five.

OLIVIA   I'm perfect just the way I am.

NORMA   That's right.

FERN   More wine?

OLIVIA   Fill 'er up.

TRICIA   Should I call Lorene?

FERN   Give her a few more minutes.

NORMA   Maybe she's having sex.

They all laugh.

OLIVIA   That's so mean.

FERN   Cliff's an improvement over.

OLIVIA   Umberto.

NORMA   The Argentinean love god.

OLIVIA   He was so handsome.

TRICIA   He stole most of her money and gave her venereal warts.

FERN   Life's a barter system. What about that Irish guy?

OLIVIA   The pipefitter who wrote poetry.

NORMA   What was his name?

TRICIA   Liam?

FERN   Laurence?

NORMA   Lance.

TRICIA   Lance right.

FERN   Their son was beautiful.

OLIVIA   Simba.

NORMA   I'm pretty sure they didn't name the kid Simba.

TRICIA   Shame about the pipefitter poet's commitment issues.

NORMA   I always liked her first husband. The one she had Diana with.

OLIVIA   What was his name?

TRICIA   Smart guy. Great hair.

FERN   Worked out. Big arms.

TRICIA   Oh for—we were her bridesmaids.

FERN   He was her first great love.

OLIVIA   The only Jewish guy she got involved with.

TRICIA   It's right on the tip of my mind.

FERN   Mannie.

NORMA   Mannie.

OLIVIA   Mannie was great. He went to court and got custody.

TRICIA   And Lorene had that seven year depression.

NORMA   She managed two affairs a marriage and a son during that depression.

*LORENE **enters.***

LORENE   Hola.

OLIVIA   About time.

FERN   Are you alright?

LORENE   Peachy.

TRICIA   You seem.

LORENE   Fine.

NORMA   Hungry?

LORENE   No. Happy birthday.

NORMA   Thank you.

OLIVIA   You look sad.

LORENE   I'm fine.

FERN   Really?

LORENE   Sure. Who's mixing?

OLIVIA   What's your poison?

LORENE   Vodka. Lots.

TRICIA   I can pick you up.

FERN   How?

> TRICIA *produces a small package of cocaine.*

TRICIA   Who wants to do some blow?

NORMA   Really?

TRICIA   Sure.

FERN   I do.

OLIVIA   Fern?!

LORENE   I'm in.

OLIVIA   Girls you could at least pretend to be shocked.

FERN   What? I haven't done cocaine in decades.

TRICIA   It's really clean.

NORMA   Well if it's really clean.

OLIVIA   Prominent pediatricians do not do cocaine.

NORMA   What fantasy world do you live in? Line 'em up.

> TRICIA *cuts coke into lines.*

TRICIA   Let's get crazy ladies.

LORENE   Everyone needs to party once in a while.

OLIVIA   It's illegal.

          OLIVIA refills her glass again.

TRICIA   So is smoking pot.

OLIVIA   But it's less—what creepy people do.

LORENE   We're in a private dining room.

OLIVIA   But I have such a delightful dinner planned.

          LORENE hands OLIVIA a straw.

LORENE   Shut up and snort.

OLIVIA   No.

NORMA   Well I will.

          NORMA grabs the straw from OLIVIA and does a fast line.

TRICIA   Whoa girl!

OLIVIA   Norma.

FERN   Now me.

FERN grabs the straw from NORMA and does a line.

TRICIA   Isn't this so fifteen years ago?

NORMA   Oh yeah.

OLIVIA   It is.

NORMA   Hmpph.

FERN   Ouch.

TRICIA   Give me the straw.

FERN   Is it supposed to hurt this much?

TRICIA   That's the garbage they cut it with.

NORMA   I thought it was clean.

TRICIA   It is. Except for the baby laxative and Drano.

FERN   My sinuses.

LORENE   It'll stop. Relax.

FERN   Hoo boy.

TRICIA does a line.

OLIVIA   I need more wine.

NORMA   Fill me up too.

FERN   Is my face okay?

TRICIA   Hoo haw.

LORENE   It's very smooth once you get over that initial rush.

TRICIA   Jesus.

NORMA   Where did you get this anyway?

TRICIA   My dealer.

FERN   You have a dealer?

TRICIA   Usually just for pot and painkillers.

OLIVIA   Who needs more wine?

NORMA   Please. Pot and painkillers?

TRICIA   For my heavy days.

FERN   I feel nice now.

NORMA   What an excellent birthday surprise.

TRICIA   Do you feel better now?

LORENE   Yeah for a second I almost forgot—

TRICIA   What's wrong?

LORENE   Nothing I —

OLIVIA   What?

LORENE   I'm leaving Clifford.

NORMA   What happened?

LORENE   He — *(pause)* wants kids.

NORMA   Kids?

TRICIA   But he's —

LORENE   I know but I don't care. We both drink too much and
                when I feel like it I go down on him and vice versa.
                What could be better right? And then we start hang-
                ing out with my best friend Brent at the agency and
                his partner Harold the fireman.

FERN   Oh oh.

LORENE   And Brent and Harold are having a kid with a surro-
                gate and they're dealing with an adoption agency and
                someone's sister is carrying her brother's fetus — which
                I find really creepy — and then bingo they have three
                kids. Honest. Three kids in six months or something.
                And all of a sudden Clifford's all I wish we had kids
                and I'm like WHAT and he says we should have real sex

and I say for god's sake Clifford if I'd wanted someone to really fuck me I wouldn't have married a bottom!

TRICIA   Oh dear.

LORENE   And now he's moving in with them and he's gonna be their live-in nanny and help them raise their future kids with the super brains—and I'm single once again.

FERN   Lorene.

NORMA   I'm so sorry.

LORENE   Got any more coke?

TRICIA   Help yourself.

OLIVIA   Could you even have a baby?

LORENE   Are you kidding? They can plant the little fuckers inside of us any time they want to. If your womb's too old they'll replace it with a sheep's womb. If you can't lactate they'll give you the nipples of a fertile sow.

FERN   I never felt better in my life than when I was breast-feeding. It was wonderful. It really was.

LORENE   My nipples turned black cracked and bled. Who needs another line?

NORMA   Me.

FERN   I often miss the way I felt when I was lactating.

LORENE   I won't have another child to resent me.

OLIVIA   Oh I'm sure little Diana and—Simba.

NORMA   Steven?

LORENE   Sammy.

NORMA,
OLIVIA
& TRICIA   SAMMY.

OLIVIA   Are fine with their empty childhoods. More wine?

LORENE   They hate me and they're teenagers now.

TRICIA   Come on. We're here to celebrate.

NORMA   My fiftieth.

LORENE   And my impending divorce.

FERN   Will he want palimony?

LORENE   They all want palimony.

NORMA   Celebrating.

OLIVIA   We should eat soon.

LORENE   I couldn't dream of it.

TRICIA   I've lost my appetite too.

NORMA   I need more wine.

OLIVIA   But we have braised—

FERN   Later.

TRICIA   Did we order champagne? It would be great to have some champagne.

OLIVIA   We're having champagne after dessert.

TRICIA   Dessert?

LORENE   As if.

NORMA   Is there any cocaine left?

OLIVIA   Hey I spent the whole goddamn month putting this stupid fucking thing together—getting the room planning the menu consulting with the chef and making sure everything would be just perfect and you're ruining it.

TRICIA   Lorene's marriage is falling apart.

OLIVIA   She married a homo.

FERN   Crisises change things.

LORENE   I don't mean to be a burden.

NORMA   It might not be a bad idea to—

OLIVIA   I'll get the maître d'.

TRICIA   Olivia wait.

NORMA   No maître d'.

OLIVIA   Shut up. Sit in your places.

FERN   But I need to—

OLIVIA   Everyone sit down.

TRICIA   Stop it.

            OLIVIA slaps TRICIA across the face.

OLIVIA   I SAID SIT DOWN!

            Pause.

TRICIA   You fucking bitch.

OLIVIA   It was an accident.

TRICIA   I can't believe it. You actually.

            Pause.

Happy birthday Norma.

TRICIA exits. Pause.

OLIVIA   More wine?

FERN   I'm good. I should—I have to go.

OLIVIA   But dinner.

FERN   I'm not hungry. Thanx. Happy birthday Norma.

FERN exits quickly.

OLIVIA   Lorene?

LORENE   You hit her.

OLIVIA   It was the coke.

LORENE   You didn't do any coke.

OLIVIA   Lorene—

LORENE   Happy birthday Norma. Sorry if I tried to make it all about me.

LORENE exits. Pause.

OLIVIA   I'm eating everything. I don't care.

NORMA   Good for you.

OLIVIA   Don't.

NORMA   What?

OLIVIA   I can hear that tone in your voice.

NORMA   No.

OLIVIA   Who else would put up with your love of bad movies?

NORMA   I'll bite. Who?

OLIVIA   You're high.

NORMA   Let's eat.

A light rises on TRICIA *alone.*

TRICIA   Annabelle Stanko. She was this greasy dark-eyed fleabag in my grade two class. She caught me peeing outside during recess once and threatened to tell the nuns unless I gave her one of my Lemon Cheez sandwiches every day. I hated her. Her father was a drunk and her mother was a fat ugly bitch everyone laughed at. No one ever played with her. I think extorting that sandwich out of me every day kinda made me her friend. Then one day everyone was talking about how Annabelle's mother was found dead with her head in the oven while her husband and children slept. She came to the school later that day to get her stuff and even though she looked vacant and tired I still said I'm glad your crazy mother killed herself. She barely looked at me. It was like she was sleepwalking. She said but now she can't protect me from him and kind of half stumbled out of the room. She never came back to school again.

FERN and LORENE join her.

LORENE   And that's why you never let anything go?

TRICIA   I'd see her occasionally. Always at that shitty shack they lived in. Taking care of her brothers and sisters like she was the mother now. The whole town knew.

FERN   So what do we do about Olivia?

TRICIA   Are either of you interested in continuing the friendship like this?

Pause.

FERN   I can't deal with another one of those scenes.

LORENE   Shouldn't Norma do something?

TRICIA   I think she thinks she is.

LORENE   Jeez.

Pause.

TRICIA   Either we care enough to do this or we don't.

LORENE   When you put it that way.

FERN   What other choice have we got?

          A light rises on OLIVIA *as she gets ready for work. By the end of her speech she's gotten dressed and taken a number of drinks.*

OLIVIA   If I could sleep. It'd be better if I could sleep. I mean I fall asleep alright but three hours later I'm swimming toward waking up and thinking no no no not yet—and then it's just—lying there—sleeping—not sleeping—suspended—listening to Norma snore—and I know a drink will help. So I take one or four. And they buy me a few more hours and kill any dreams—I hate my dreams—and then I go to work. But if I could sleep all night I think it would be alright then. If I could just have a full night's sleep.

          OLIVIA *exits the house to find* TRICIA, LORENE *and* FERN *waiting for her.*

TRICIA   Good morning.

OLIVIA   Hey.

LORENE   Got a minute?

OLIVIA   At seven fifteen? In my driveway?

FERN   You haven't had anything to drink have you?

OLIVIA   Of course not.

LORENE   Liv?

OLIVIA   It's none of your fucking business.

LORENE   We treasure and support you.

FERN   You know that.

TRICIA   But you're an alcoholic and you need to get help.

OLIVIA   Oh please—one night when you all get high on coke and things get a little out of control and all of a sudden everyone's interventing Olivia.

LORENE   This has nothing to do with the cocaine.

FERN   It has to do with the way you drink.

TRICIA   And the things you do and say when you're drunk.

OLIVIA   Get out of my way.

TRICIA   Not until you've heard us out.

OLIVIA   Fern Lorene why do you guys let her talk you into these things? You know she only does it to prove she has control.

FERN   It's not about Tricia.

LORENE   Or control.

OLIVIA   Yes it is. Everything's about Tricia. And control. Now if you don't mind I have to—

TRICIA   Puke on me? Hit me?

OLIVIA   Fuck off okay. Just fuck off and stay the fuck away from me. I don't need this shit.

TRICIA   If you get in your car I'll call the cops and tell them you've been drinking.

OLIVIA   But I haven't—

TRICIA   Then you've got nothing to worry about if they give you a breathalyzer test.

OLIVIA   You all drink with me.

FERN   We don't slap you.

TRICIA   What's so hideous in your life that you have to drink like this?

OLIVIA   Nothing.

LORENE   Tell us what you need.

OLIVIA   Look why don't we talk about this after I get off work. I'm going to be late.

TRICIA   No.

OLIVIA   I'll get Norma.

FERN   Leave Norma out of this.

OLIVIA   I'm not an alcoholic.

FERN   I can smell the booze from here.

OLIVIA   At least I never married a fag or let five guys fuck me
              in one night or was—was boring.

TRICIA   Stop it.

OLIVIA   We all have addictions why are mine suddenly so
              important?

FERN   Because you're unhappy and you're hurting yourself
              and it hurts us to watch you do it.

OLIVIA   I'm NOT unhappy! You're the unhappy ones. You're all
              way unhappier than me. We—we should get Norma.

TRICIA   Norma's your enabler.

OLIVIA   Leave me alone!

FERN   Why are you so angry?

OLIVIA   I don't know okay. I don't fucking know. It just—I
              never really cared—a shot here and there—I don't

know—it makes me feel better—alcohol likes me. It likes me a lot. And I just. Stop okay. Just stop. I need to—go away okay. Just go away now.

TRICIA No.

OLIVIA Lorene you know me. It's just a phase—a thing—

LORENE Olivia you've been doing this for years.

FERN There are people.

LORENE Who can help.

OLIVIA Help what?

TRICIA Help you quit drinking.

OLIVIA I don't want to quit drinking.

TRICIA You have to.

OLIVIA But you're my friends.

FERN You don't treat us like friends.

OLIVIA I do. I love—

TRICIA slaps OLIVIA across the face.

TRICIA You're not just a drunk you're a boring drunk.

Long pause.

LORENE   You have to stop.

OLIVIA   I'll die.

FERN   You won't.

LORENE   I know how strong you are.

OLIVIA   But Norma.

LORENE   Norma wants you to be healthy too.

OLIVIA   I don't think I —

FERN   You can.

LORENE   Just give it a try.

TRICIA   There's a place we can take you where people will help
             you. If you want to go. You have to want to go.

OLIVIA   A place?

TRICIA   For rehabilitation.

FERN   There are professionals there.

LORENE   They'll help you.

OLIVIA   Stop?

TRICIA   Yes.

              Pause.

OLIVIA   You'd take me there?

FERN   And we'll come and see you every day.

OLIVIA   Seriously?

TRICIA   If we can.

LORENE   If it'll help.

OLIVIA   I could stop?

TRICIA   Yes.

              NORMA enters.

NORMA   What's going on?

OLIVIA   They're interventing me.

NORMA   Get out of here.

TRICIA   No.

OLIVIA   They say there's a place that'll help.

FERN   Norma you know she needs help.

NORMA   I can't believe you'd do this.

TRICIA   I can't believe you wouldn't.

           Pause.

OLIVIA   Norma please?

NORMA   What?

FERN   Don't you want her to quit?

NORMA   Of course.

LORENE   Take the step.

OLIVIA   Norma?

           Pause.

NORMA   It's entirely up to you.

           Slow fade to black.

ACT TWO

Lights up on NORMA *making herself a cup of tea as* FERN, *carrying her own mug, joins her.*

FERN   It's hard to be on your own after so many years.

NORMA   I'm okay.

FERN   Norma.

NORMA   It was unnecessary.

FERN   You can start visiting her soon.

NORMA   For an hour. Twice a week.

FERN   The months will fly by. We're lucky to have gotten her in such a great facility so quickly.

NORMA   Right.

FERN   I just don't understand how you could let it get so—

NORMA   It's none of your business.

FERN   You're an intelligent person. You know when something's wrong.

NORMA   I can deal with her.

FERN   But you couldn't keep her from attacking Tricia.

NORMA   Tricia asks for everything she gets.

FERN   Those two are always at each other.

NORMA   They're too much alike.

FERN   Not really. They're more opposite. It's almost like—

NORMA   What?

FERN   Like you need both of them to make the relationship work.

NORMA   Leave the psychology to the professionals Fern.

FERN   I'm sorry. You're right. I'm a bit.

NORMA   Forget it.

FERN   I know how hard this is for you.

Pause.

NORMA   She's all I ever wanted.

FERN   You've never woken up and looked at her sleeping and thought what the fuck have I done with my life?

NORMA   No. Never. Have you?

FERN   Not maybe no okay once or twice in twenty-three years.

NORMA   That's normal.

FERN   Then why haven't you done it?

NORMA   Because I'm not normal. Fern you don't have to babysit me.

FERN   Should I go? Do you want me to go? I'll go.

NORMA   Are you okay?

FERN   No I'm just yes okay but it's not anything big really. Really.

NORMA   What?

FERN   Do you promise not to tell anyone? You know. Doctor-patient confidentiality even though you're not really my doctor.

NORMA   Of course. What is it?

FERN   I've been there's this it's uh I've been having an affair.

NORMA   With who?

FERN   Barry.

NORMA   From across the street?

FERN   Yes.

NORMA   Husband of Hoohah?

FERN   Linda. You can't tell anyone.

NORMA   For how long?

FERN   Thirteen years.

NORMA   Thirteen years? Jesus. Most people don't stay married that long.

FERN   I know. I just.

NORMA   Do you love him?

FERN   I love certain things about him. Like with Walt.

NORMA   Why are you spilling this now?

FERN   The stupid bastard wants us to leave our partners to
          be together.

NORMA   Why?

FERN   I don't know. Men.

NORMA   You're the one with the marriage and kids and all the
          stuff we're supposed to be jealous of.

FERN   It was just so—Walt was working more and more. We
          didn't talk as much. Nothing hostile or anything we
          just didn't have as much to say. And then one day I
          needed some construction paper or something for
          one of Miles's art projects and I went over and Barry
          was working on this silly ad for a pizza place and he'd
          drawn this very sexy woman that he said made him
          think of me and I laughed and said I don't look like
          that and he said you do to me and then all of a sudden
          it's like—I don't know—we're kissing and we're like
          two drowning people trying to suck the last bit of air
          from the other's lungs and it just just just happened.
          Hard and fast and wonderful on the floor of his studio.

NORMA   Yow.

FERN   When it was over he gave me a clean painting cloth
          to wipe myself with and our hands touched and I said
          we can never do this again.

NORMA   But you did.

FERN   Twice a week. Always in his studio. Always in the afternoon. I kept telling myself I wouldn't go back.

NORMA   Why did you?

FERN   For the way he smelled.

NORMA   Really?

FERN   I can't describe it. It was just this faint trace of very specific male B.O. that drove me crazy.

NORMA   And?

FERN   Walt has a lovely penis but Barry's—it's not that big or anything—it's just the way it's shaped and the way we both fit together so perfectly. Like a—a key in a lock. He opens me up. It gives me great pleasure. I have no control—you know?

NORMA   Penises aren't really my aisle.

FERN   You mean you've never.

NORMA   I am a lesbian.

FERN   Right. Of course. I just never really. Sorry. Of course. What was I thinking? But wow. Really? Sorry.

NORMA   What are you going to do?

FERN   I have no idea. Please don't tell anyone. I shouldn't've
            even told you. I just—I'm so scared. I love my life. I
            love my children. I don't want it to change. But Barry's
            so—he's gotten more intense since his kids went away
            to school and Linda got that promotion.

NORMA   And you're sure Walt has no idea?

FERN   He's never given me the slightest indication of any
            suspicion.

NORMA   How would he react?

FERN   He could go through the roof he could not care he
            could cry—I have no idea and that really really both-
            ers me too.

NORMA   Do either of these men make you happy?

FERN   Happy? I don't know. They make things—alright. How
            did this happen? I'm sorry. I had no right to dump this
            on you. Especially now.

NORMA   It's a relief to talk about someone else actually.

            Pause.

FERN   Do you need anything before I go?

NORMA   I'm fine. Thank you.

FERN   You're welcome.

FERN gives NORMA a hug.

Things will get better. You'll see.

NORMA Sure.

A light rises on TRICIA and LORENE in a waiting room.

LORENE Should this be taking so long?

TRICIA She has to do her exit interview.

Pause.

Did you ever hear from your father after he left?

LORENE Never. Why?

TRICIA You don't talk about your family.

LORENE My mother had no heart and my father had no soul. The end.

TRICIA Grandparents?

LORENE That I knew? On my mother's side. Holocaust survivors who hated everyone and everything. Who could blame them? But not exactly fun city for a kid right. Why?

TRICIA It just occurred to me that after all these years there's still a lot I don't know about you.

LORENE   It's the here and now that matters.

TRICIA   Amen.

    FERN enters.

LORENE   Where were you?

FERN   I had to drop Donnie off at football practice then Miles needed a ride to work and Blake had to go to a friend's. I swear I have done nothing but fucking drive kids around for eighteen years.

TRICIA   And yoga.

FERN   I'd be bugshit crazy otherwise. Where's Olivia?

LORENE   Still waiting?

TRICIA   Who are we gonna get when she walks out of those doors?

FERN   It's been so long since I thought of her as anything but a sad drunk.

    A buzzer sounds.

LORENE   Omigod.

    OLIVIA enters carrying a suitcase. Pause.

TRICIA   Hi.

OLIVIA   Did I ever tell you how wonderful you were as Ophelia?

TRICIA   Never.

OLIVIA   I really can't thank you enough for what you were willing to do to help me.

TRICIA   Really?

OLIVIA   It took real love to do what you did.

OLIVIA goes to TRICIA and hugs her tightly.

Thank you. All of you.

LORENE and FERN join in the hug. Lights rise on NORMA setting food on the table.

NORMA   Waldorf salad with a creamy blue cheese dressing. Prime rib medium rare. Baked potato sour cream bacon bits butter creamed corn white bread milk. Perfect. Absolutely perfect.

OLIVIA enters with luggage.

OLIVIA   I'm home.

Pause.

NORMA   Hello.

OLIVIA   Hello.

Pause.

The girls decided not to come up.

NORMA   I made dinner.

OLIVIA   Smells wonderful.

NORMA   Are you—

OLIVIA   I really—

They rush into one another's arms and kiss, holding one another very tight.

Norma.

NORMA   I missed you so much.

OLIVIA   I thought about you every day.

NORMA   Every minute.

They kiss again. NORMA *pulls away.*

I wanted to have all your favourites perfectly made when you came home.

OLIVIA   Thank you.

NORMA   Milk?

OLIVIA   Water please.

NORMA   Water?

OLIVIA   Please.

NORMA gets OLIVIA a glass of water as they speak.

NORMA   You look wonderful.

OLIVIA   You too.

NORMA   Please. I haven't had a good night's sleep in months.
             I'm hideous.

OLIVIA   You're not. Thank you.

NORMA   Your skin looks so different.

OLIVIA   I can't tell you how different I feel.

NORMA sits.

NORMA   Of course I've spoken to your counsellor.

OLIVIA   I don't want to drink anymore Norma.

NORMA   I understand.

OLIVIA   I'm going to use AA to stay clean.

NORMA   Good.

OLIVIA   I'm hoping you might come to a few meetings with me. Just so you know what's going on.

NORMA   Sure. Right.

OLIVIA   It'll seem strange at first.

NORMA   No doubt.

OLIVIA   It'll take time for us to get to know each other sober.

NORMA   Naturally.

OLIVIA   But it really works.

NORMA   Whatever you need.

OLIVIA   Thank you.

　　　　　Pause.

NORMA   You should eat.

OLIVIA   I'll have some salad.

NORMA   Prime rib. Medium rare. Just the way you like it.

OLIVIA   It looks divine.

NORMA   What?

OLIVIA   Nothing it's just—at the centre—we were kept on a pretty strict diet—no sugar no fat—

NORMA   You said you thought you were going to die.

OLIVIA   I had the worst headaches and stomach cramps for nearly a month.

NORMA   The sour cream will fix that.

OLIVIA   But then it wasn't so bad and I guess I kind of got used to the food.

NORMA   Really?

OLIVIA   Certain ingredients—I'm sure they're a trigger for me.

NORMA   So let me know what those things are and I'll learn to cook around them.

OLIVIA   I've got a whole list in a box with my affirmations—

NORMA   Affirmations?

OLIVIA   Little prayers I say every day to help stay sober.

NORMA   Right.

OLIVIA   Actually I thought—if you're alright with it—I might take over some of the cooking sometime.

      Pause.

NORMA   You?

OLIVIA   I've got some recipes—

NORMA   In your affirmation box.

OLIVIA   That's right. Salmon chicken breast tofu.

NORMA   Did you just say tofu?

OLIVIA   Yeah can you believe it?

NORMA   I thought you were joking.

OLIVIA   You okay?

NORMA   Sure.

OLIVIA   It's just that—well you're a doctor—I don't have to tell you about all the horrible things they're discovering about meat-based diets. Cholesterol cancer all of that.

NORMA   Are you a vegetarian?

OLIVIA   Of course not.

         Pause.

NORMA   I guess I can clear these dishes then.

OLIVIA   I'm just going to step outside for a minute.

NORMA   Why?

OLIVIA   I'm going to—smoke a cigarette.

NORMA   What?

OLIVIA   I just have a few a day.

NORMA   Cigarettes?

OLIVIA   At least I'm not drinking myself to death anymore
right? Everyone at the centre smoked. Don't worry.
It's temporary.

> *OLIVIA exits.*

NORMA   Right.

> *NORMA clears the table as a light rises on LORENE dressing to go out.*

LORENE   The thing is I almost immediately slept a lot better.
Clifford was a lovely guy and it was so great to cuddle
with him but I always had this nagging fear that he'd
wake and see how ugly I am when I'm unconscious.
Isn't that weird? I wonder if most love results from
being fucking sleep deprived.

> *Lights rise on NORMA and TRICIA in a corner of the
church basement eating doughnuts and drinking coffee.
TRICIA is seated.*

TRICIA   This doughnut has a very odd texture.

NORMA   Like sawdust with sugar.

TRICIA   Sugar?

NORMA   The coffee's terrible. How much longer do we have to stay?

TRICIA   Until Olivia gets tired of introducing Lorene and Fern to her fellow drunks.

NORMA   Why aren't you out there?

TRICIA   Had to sit down.

NORMA   Back pain?

TRICIA   How are you?

NORMA   Tired and bitchy thanx for asking.

TRICIA   It was important to Olivia we help her celebrate this three month milestone.

NORMA   So they throw her a party for achieving something the general populace does without a second thought.

TRICIA   Tell me you're not this cynical and negative around her.

NORMA   Around her I'm as positive and supportive as a dyke
           my size and age can possibly be.

TRICIA   But?

NORMA   I'm not convinced this god loving replacing of a nega-
           tive addiction with a positive one is the best course of
           action for everyone.

TRICIA   Have you got a better alternative?

NORMA   No and that's why I keep my mouth shut. But I still
           distrust the whole George Romero vibe of this place.

TRICIA   When was the last time you saw her this excited about
           anything?

NORMA   She starts everything with great enthusiasm.

TRICIA   Why don't you and I go to dinner soon—just the two
           of us? Take cabs. Gossip about people we don't like.
           Drink a bit.

NORMA   You could have at least consulted me.

TRICIA   You would've sabotaged it.

NORMA   Why would I do that?

TRICIA   Because—because sometimes I think you like her bet-
           ter when she's drunk.

NORMA   That's ridiculous.

TRICIA   It makes her—easier to control.

NORMA   Fuck you.

          LORENE enters.

LORENE   Hey—tension.

NORMA   It's late.

          FERN enters.

FERN   This reminds me of church for people who are even
           more messed up than the people who go to church.
           Everything alright?

NORMA   It's time to go.

LORENE   Apparently.

          OLIVIA enters.

OLIVIA   Wasn't this fun? I'm so glad you were all here. It means
           so much to me. I got my ninety day chip. Look.

TRICIA   That is so great.

          OLIVIA goes to NORMA and hugs her.

OLIVIA   And you cranky pants—I know how much you didn't want to do this. It's why I love you.

NORMA pulls away from OLIVIA.

NORMA   Great.

OLIVIA   And quit looking so gloomy. Right now. Smile.

NORMA smiles.

Everyone smile.

They all smile.

That's better. This is the beginning of my new life and I owe it all to you four.

FERN   Our pleasure.

LORENE   Oh wow.

NORMA   What?

LORENE   Shalimar.

TRICIA   What?

LORENE   Can't you smell it? It's so strong. Someone really—

OLIVIA   Shalimar?

LORENE's communication device sounds.

TRICIA   Do you smell it?

LORENE   Hello.

FERN   I haven't even heard someone even say Shalimar in like
           decades.

LORENE   What?

TRICIA   I can smell a great many things but not—

LORENE   Are you serious—

NORMA   Shalimar. No. Cigarette stench and B.O. Yes.

FERN   These people all reek of cigarettes.

NORMA   I got face and hair cancer just walking past the smok-
           ers at the door.

LORENE   I see. Thank you.

OLIVIA   Lorene I think you're having a stroke. We can't smell.

LORENE   My mother died.

TRICIA   Your mother wasn't dead?

           Lorene.

LORENE   That was the extended care centre. She's been a veg-
         etable there for the last eleven years. She finally died.

FERN   It's been so long since you even spoke of her—

LORENE   No.

         OLIVIA **hugs** *LORENE.*

OLIVIA   Sweetie.

         LORENE **pulls away.**

NORMA   Are you okay?

LORENE   Yeah.

TRICIA   I know you were never close to her.

FERN   Still it's your mother.

LORENE   I smelled her perfume. Just before. It filled the room.

OLIVIA   Did you drive?

LORENE   Yeah.

TRICIA   I cabbed. Let me drive you home.

LORENE   Oh no that's.

TRICIA   Shut up I'm driving come on.

LORENE   Okay. Night everyone.

          The others whisper good night to LORENE *and blow her kisses as she exits with* TRICIA.

FERN   That's so sad.

OLIVIA   She has a lot of unresolved issues there.

FERN   Losing a parent—even a bad one—is a profound experience. It took me years to get over my parents' deaths and I loved them.

NORMA   Can we go now?

OLIVIA   I'm going to help Helen stack the chairs. I'll be right out.

NORMA   The inevitable Helen.

FERN   Who?

OLIVIA   My sponsor.

FERN   Right. I have to run.

OLIVIA   Thanx again. So much.

          They kiss. FERN *exits.*

          We won't be a minute.

NORMA   Right.

> OLIVIA *moves off as a light rises on* TRICIA *and* LORENE *at a bar.*

LORENE   I'm smelling it again?

TRICIA   Really?

LORENE   Phantom Shalimar.

TRICIA   Does the scent trigger any other memories?

LORENE   Her pushing me away. That's all I remember her doing really. Don't bother me now. Later sweetie. I'm busy. That sort of thing.

TRICIA   Nice.

LORENE   Did I mention this place is a toilet?

TRICIA   That's why I like it.

LORENE   It has a certain—desperate neediness.

TRICIA   Character.

LORENE   I think the couple over there wants to kill us.

TRICIA   Or something.

LORENE   Another?

TRICIA   What do you think?

LORENE   I don't think we've hit rock bottom yet.

TRICIA   Norma's still pretty angry with me.

LORENE   She'll get over it.

TRICIA   Did she ever tell you about coming out to her parents?

LORENE   No.

TRICIA   She was eighteen and had spent the night at Olivia's—just slept there—without calling. Her dad accused her of whoring around with some boy so—even though she hadn't told Liv yet—she told him she was a lesbian.

LORENE   What happened?

TRICIA   He beat her up. Really badly.

LORENE   No.

TRICIA   Her mother told her she deserved it. She came to stay with me that night and never spoke to them again. University. Medical school. Everything. She did it herself. Both of her folks are still alive. Still in that old house on the east side. Her mother writes once in a while but Norma just ignores her.

LORENE   How could I not know that?

TRICIA   Forgiveness isn't her best trait.

          Pause.

LORENE   You ever think about being alone for the rest of your
          life?

TRICIA   Sure.

LORENE   It's the worst thing I can imagine.

TRICIA   Then you have a very limited imagination.

LORENE   A lot of people think having children means they won't
          die alone.

TRICIA   Doesn't seem to have helped your mother. Or mine.

LORENE   It's just sometimes I feel like a fat baggy old woman
          that no one will ever touch again and it makes me feel
          really really sad. Not to get laid—to wake up with
          someone's skin touching yours.

TRICIA   There'll always be men wanting to touch you Lorene.

LORENE   Hot muscular ones?

TRICIA   How rich are you?

          LORENE laughs. Pause.

LORENE   You don't get lonely?

TRICIA   Everyone does. Even Fern with Walt. Even Olivia and Norma.

LORENE   I don't think that's the same lonely as alone lonely.

TRICIA   It's just as painful.

LORENE   You're always so cool with this stuff.

TRICIA   I'm not a romantic.

LORENE   Have you ever been in love?

TRICIA   I need you so much I have to control your every move and thought in love or real in love where you just want the best for the other person?

LORENE   It was that political activist guy you nearly married right?

TRICIA   I nearly had his baby.

LORENE   What happened?

TRICIA   It wasn't a good time for a baby and we both knew it.

LORENE   You ever regret that?

TRICIA   There's no shortage of people in the world.

> *Pause.*

LORENE   I'm gonna go.

TRICIA   I thought you wanted another.

LORENE   Naw. Thanx for this.

TRICIA   No problem.

LORENE   You want a ride?

TRICIA   I think I'm going to get to know the killer couple
             thanx.

LORENE   I hope you packed your meat cleaver.

TRICIA   And some wrist restraints. Call me if you need to talk.

LORENE   I'm fine. I'm just—verklempt.

TRICIA   I'll come with you.

LORENE   No. I'm okay. Thanx.

TRICIA   Really?

LORENE   Yeah. I just feel like—being alone.

TRICIA   Sure.

> *They kiss and hug. LORENE exits. Lights rise on OLIVIA
> setting the table with containers of food. NORMA is pol-
> ishing glasses.*

NORMA   How many of these dishes are vegetarian?

OLIVIA   Some.

NORMA   Don't think I don't know.

OLIVIA   Know what?

NORMA   That you're not eating meat.

OLIVIA   I eat seafood.

NORMA   Is Helen a vegetarian?

OLIVIA   Helen eats anything. And she's straight. You know that.

NORMA   Why didn't you invite her tonight?

OLIVIA   She's spending the evening with her children. She has a life.

NORMA   And yet you spend so much time together.

OLIVIA   You don't have to be jealous.

NORMA   So you're not?

OLIVIA   What?

NORMA   Feeling attracted to her?

OLIVIA   Helen? No. Not Helen.

NORMA   Someone else?

OLIVIA   What?

NORMA   Men?

OLIVIA   What?

NORMA   Are you feeling attracted to any of them?

OLIVIA   You mean like guys at meetings?

NORMA   Yes.

OLIVIA goes to NORMA and kisses her.

OLIVIA   You want to get married?

NORMA   What?

OLIVIA   Will that make you feel more secure?

NORMA   I don't want you to marry me because you think it's
         what I want.

OLIVIA   Whatever it takes to put an end to your moping and
         jealousy.

NORMA   Excuse me?

OLIVIA   It's just—your attitude.

NORMA   I'm sorry. I'm really trying not to be a selfish bitch.
             I'm so proud of you. But it's just different you
             know—different.

             OLIVIA kisses NORMA. FERN enters.

FERN   Hiya.

NORMA   Fern?

OLIVIA   I can't believe you got here before Tricia. You okay?

FERN   Yeah don't ask. Is this Thai?

NORMA   Delivery.

FERN   Wow. How are you doing?

OLIVIA   Some days I wake up and it's not so great but some days
             I wake up and it's amazing but I hardly ever wake up
             wishing I was dead anymore.

FERN   That's—good.

NORMA   However she is smoking nearly a package of cigarettes
             a day.

OLIVIA   Don't rat me out to company dear.

             LORENE enters.

LORENE   Hey all.

NORMA   Welcome.

LORENE   Where's Tricia?

OLIVIA   I don't know but I left six messages so she'd know it
          was important.

LORENE   Has anyone spoken to her recently?

FERN   She's been very hard to get hold of.

OLIVIA   Trish gets busy with something and she disappears.

FERN   Do you think she's upset because she didn't win that
          award?

LORENE   She was fine with it.

FERN   What are we drinking?

NORMA   We have a stunning array of sparkling waters as well as
          sugar and chemical loaded soft drinks that are almost
          guaranteed to prove carcinogenic or give you a stroke.

FERN   Excellent.

OLIVIA   I bought some vodka coolers.

FERN   What?

LORENE   You went into a liquor store?

OLIVIA   Sure.

NORMA   You know that's not allowed.

OLIVIA   It didn't bother me a bit. Just because I can't drink anymore doesn't mean you girls can't. They're in the fridge. Help yourself.

FERN   I wouldn't feel right.

LORENE   Anyway I've come to kind of enjoy these booze pot substance-free get-togethers.

FERN   Me too.

LORENE   Anything with sugar is good for me.

        TRICIA enters.

TRICIA   Sorry I'm late.

OLIVIA   Are you—?

TRICIA   What?

OLIVIA   Alright?

TRICIA   I have to sit down.

NORMA   You okay?

TRICIA   Be a pooch and get me a diet whatever would you?

FERN   Tricia you look.

TRICIA   I'm fine.

OLIVIA   Have a cooler.

TRICIA   No thanx. What's the big occasion?

OLIVIA   Well we haven't gotten together since Lorene buried her mom. So I wanted us all to get together tonight to say that even though we're not your family we're here for you.

         Pause.

LORENE   Wow. Thank you. Really.

TRICIA   Very lovely gesture.

NORMA   Birthdays aren't the only excuse to get together.

FERN   So what's on the menu?

NORMA   Tamarind shrimp pad Thai cashew chicken—

OLIVIA   And a buncha other shit. Help yourselves.

FERN   I'm starving.

NORMA   Me too.

LORENE   Ooh look at the shrimp.

TRICIA takes a pill bottle out of her bag and takes two.

FERN   What are you taking?

TRICIA   Percocets.

LORENE   You're in pain?

TRICIA   Almost constantly.

NORMA   It's stenosis isn't it?

TRICIA   The cartilage between my discs is breaking down and I'm developing bone spurs that block the nerve endings to my lower body.

LORENE   This is sounding serious.

NORMA   Symptoms are stiffness and pain—

TRICIA   Pain and more pain—

LORENE   How long has this been going on?

TRICIA   The last couple years—it started with a tingling in my lower back—then it started waking me up at night. If I sat in the same position for more than ten minutes it started. Walking got harder.

LORENE   Is there a surgery or something?

TRICIA   Maybe but they could hit my spinal cord and cripple me for life.

OLIVIA   Tricia.

TRICIA   I just don't have the energy to hide it anymore.

FERN   You should've said something.

TRICIA   The only power I've ever had is to walk away if I have to—leave—take off under my own steam no matter where I am or who I'm with. The idea of that being taken away.

OLIVIA   Horrifying.

TRICIA   Middle age is an endless parade of what the fuck.

    Pause.

LORENE   We're here.

TRICIA   There are times when it's not so bad.

FERN   Anything you need—we'll do it.

TRICIA   And other times I can't even walk a block.

OLIVIA   Just call.

TRICIA   Someone make me a small plate.

LORENE   What would you like?

TRICIA   A mouthful of everything.

FERN   Thai. I feel so exotic.

NORMA   Or something.

LORENE   You don't approve?

NORMA   I like to cook.

OLIVIA   This is so much healthier.

NORMA   Healthier?

OLIVIA   Nothing's made with butter.

NORMA   You smoke cigarettes.

OLIVIA   Everyone's allowed one vice.

NORMA   It's not a vice. It's a filthy disgusting addiction that
           hooks and kills as many if not more people than alco-
           hol and it makes me sick.

OLIVIA   I didn't realize it bothered you so much.

NORMA   Remember how I used to banish Tricia from the house
           when she smoked and now I've got you climbing into
           bed reeking of tobacco—

OLIVIA   Which is so much worse than when I used to crawl into bed reeking of alcohol?

NORMA   Sorry. I forgot I'm not supposed to rock the boat. Anything Olivia does is fine as long as it's not drinking. I apologize.

         Pause.

LORENE   I think I will have one of those coolers.

TRICIA   Get me one too.

FERN   With the drugs?

TRICIA   Oh yeah.

         LORENE gets coolers as they speak.

LORENE   On the good news side of things I've made the first move in re-establishing contact with Diana and Sammy.

FERN   Seriously?

LORENE   I just dropped their fathers a line suggesting that if the kids have any questions they want answered or whatever I'm open to that. And if not I'm fine with that too.

TRICIA   Why?

LORENE   I want them to know that my absence in their life
           wasn't because of them.

NORMA   Have you heard anything?

LORENE   No thank god. I was so terrified they might actually
           take me up on it. Ha!

                    They all laugh. Pause.

FERN   Olivia the food is excellent.

OLIVIA   Tissue—more?

TRICIA   I'm fine.

                    *TRICIA takes another pill out of her purse and washes it
                    down with the cooler.*

LORENE   What's that now?

TRICIA   Stool softener. To offset the painkillers which bung
           me up like you wouldn't believe.

LORENE   Charming.

TRICIA   It's like *Valley of the Dolls* with rectal fissures.

NORMA   Can you still write?

TRICIA   For about an hour a day. If I'm high enough.

LORENE   You have to let us know when you need help.

OLIVIA   I think we should come up with some kind of schedule.

TRICIA   What?

OLIVIA   To take care of you. Someone to vacuum on Monday take you to the store on Wednesday do your banking on Friday—

FERN   Is that what you'd like?

TRICIA   I'd sooner die. Look I told you about this—

OLIVIA   *(cutting her off)* Because you need help. I get it—

TRICIA   No. Stop. Okay. I wanted you to be aware of what's happening but I don't need anyone taking over my life—

OLIVIA   Don't be afraid to admit you're powerless over the pain.

TRICIA *downs the last of her cooler.*

TRICIA   I won't. Now can I trouble someone for a ride home?

NORMA   Already?

TRICIA   Yeah.

LORENE   I go right by your place.

FERN   You sure because I can.

LORENE   No sweat. Do you need to go right now?

TRICIA   Yeah. It's the drugs. Sorry.

            LORENE abandons the partially finished cooler.

LORENE   Let's go then.

NORMA   Do you need help getting to the car?

TRICIA   I'm fine with short distances.

FERN   I guess I'll go too.

LORENE   Norma Livy this was so thoughtful. Thank you.

NORMA   Our pleasure.

            Hugs and kisses all around.

OLIVIA   Tissue don't hesitate to call us.

TRICIA   I won't.

NORMA   Good night.

            *TRICIA, LORENE and FERN exit. Pause as OLIVIA begins
            to clear plates. NORMA helps her.*

            Sorry about the cigarette thing.

OLIVIA   You're absolutely right of course. If I have the will-
            power to quit drinking and overeating I should have
            the willpower to quit smoking.

NORMA   Nothing says you have to be perfect.

OLIVIA   Norma that thing we were talking about before every-
            one arrived.

NORMA   Yes?

OLIVIA   All these new feelings and sensations. It's really hard
            to tell what's real and what's just novelty you know.

                    Pause.

NORMA   Is there someone you're attracted to?

OLIVIA   At the meetings.

NORMA   Who?

OLIVIA   Just this guy.

                    Pause.

            We've never done anything but shake hands and chat.
            But he's so nice to me and the way he smiles.

NORMA   Stop. Please.

OLIVIA   I'm sorry.

NORMA   I can't. I have to. Jesus.

          NORMA sits.

OLIVIA   I love you. You know I love you. But things I thought I thought I think maybe I don't think them anymore and I don't get it.

NORMA   I've supported you. I've put up with—with—everything.

OLIVIA   Nothing happened okay. I just—I felt I should tell you.

NORMA   Why?

OLIVIA   You're my partner.

NORMA   All I can think of is that weird phone call I got from your mom just after you moved in here—with her sobbing and saying Olivia promised she'd stay with me forever.

OLIVIA   She was senile and in an extended care home. I made a promise to you. You made one to me.

NORMA   What am I supposed to say?

OLIVIA   Say it's alright. Say you understand.

NORMA   You're not the person I've been waking up with for all these years.

OLIVIA   It's like every minute of my life I'm trying to stay positive and strong and the whole time this thing inside of me is saying just have a fucking drink.

NORMA   I know.

OLIVIA   I see that cooler sitting there and I can practically taste it.

NORMA   I know.

OLIVIA   It takes every ounce of my willpower not to finish it.

NORMA   I know.

OLIVIA   I can give up booze and I can give up cigarettes but I can't give up Norma after thirty odd years. I can't.

NORMA   And I can't give up Olivia.

OLIVIA   But I don't want to fail.

NORMA   I know.

OLIVIA   Because if I do everything will just go back to the way it was before.

NORMA   I know.

    Long pause.

You know I've always loved you no matter what.

OLIVIA   I do.

NORMA   And I always will. No matter what.

OLIVIA   I can smell the vodka under the lemon.

NORMA   Nothing can take my love away.

OLIVIA   I think I'm cured. I really do. I think I could have just one or two drinks and stop. Like a normal person.

NORMA   Really?

OLIVIA   Absolutely. The program's really helped me.

        OLIVIA moves into NORMA's arms.

NORMA   You've been a very good girl.

OLIVIA   It's just the end of a cooler.

NORMA   And then we'll go to bed. No one will ever know.

        NORMA picks up the cooler.

OLIVIA   Just one drink.

NORMA   You're strong.

OLIVIA   Norma.

NORMA   It's okay.

NORMA gives OLIVIA a long drink from the bottle, like a baby.

OLIVIA   I love you.

NORMA   I love you too.

OLIVIA drinks greedily as a light rises on FERN.

FERN   He cried when I told him. The tears were pretty hard to take. And he's such a wonderful guy. But I told him I have a family. They have to come first. What we've been doing these last thirteen years is wrong and it's going to stop now. He said he loved me. I said I didn't care. We didn't kiss or touch. He nodded and I walked away. And now it's like this—endless tugging somewhere deep inside. Something that's missing. This ache. It was only an hour twice a week but missing it makes me feel so fucking—empty. Walt's even been concerned enough to ask if I'm depressed. That never happens. I never get depressed. Walt never notices. It's like this craving.

A light rises on LORENE setting a table at TRICIA's home. TRICIA sits in a chair glaring at her.

TRICIA   I don't feel like a party.

LORENE   Our birthdays are so close together. Two birds one stone.

TRICIA   What's to celebrate?

LORENE   Fern's always running the boys somewhere. Norma and Olivia never call. I'm working twice as hard for half the money. We need to do this.

TRICIA   You need to do this.

LORENE   You might be perfectly happy to turn fifty alone but I'm not.

TRICIA   Because you haven't found a new husband yet?

LORENE   Don't.

TRICIA   Sorry. I'm.

     Pause.

LORENE   I got a call from Diana right after the bottom fell out of the real estate market. She wanted to meet for a coffee. She's getting married and planning on having children and felt it was important to know something about where she came from. I told her about my mother my grandparents—I wouldn't say Diana was sympathetic exactly but she did seem to understand. She was so much like Mannie but her eyes were mine. And her mouth. It was so strange—seeing someone else with my smile.

TRICIA   Did you bring any alcohol for this do?

LORENE   Just pizza and pop.

TRICIA   I have some bourbon in the pantry.

LORENE   Do you want a drink? You seem a little moody.

TRICIA   The paper killed my column last week.

LORENE   What?

TRICIA   They dumped a bunch of us old-timers.

LORENE   You should've said something.

TRICIA   If it was important someone would've noticed.

LORENE   Did they offer you something online?

TRICIA   Yeah for buttons but honestly the writing's shit these days anyway. There's something about being in constant pain that everyone finds boring. You want some?

LORENE   Pour me a shot. Someone will snap you up.

TRICIA   What dream world do you live in?

LORENE   But you must have insurance or disability—

TRICIA   Long-term freelancer. No benefits.

LORENE   Savings?

TRICIA   No.

LORENE   I had no idea.

TRICIA   Please don't mention it to the others.

LORENE   You know any one of us will help in any way—

        FERN enters.

FERN   Happy birthday boiday girls.

LORENE   Thanx.

TRICIA   You look terrible.

FERN   Why thank you.

LORENE   Something to drink?

FERN   Anything real.

TRICIA   Bourbon.

FERN   Oh yeah.

        TRICIA pours FERN a drink.

TRICIA   Here you go.

FERN   Thanx. Real quick before the lesbians arrive.

LORENE   Have you spoken to them?

FERN Not for a few weeks. You?

LORENE No.

FERN Trish?

TRICIA No.

LORENE Maybe they're not coming.

TRICIA Who cares?

FERN *(raises her glass)* To fifty. Again.

LORENE Cheers.

TRICIA Yeah.

They all drink. Pause.

Why do you keep touching your shoulder?

FERN I overextended a tendon and it's still healing.

TRICIA You hurt yourself doing yoga?

FERN My doctor suggested I take a break for a while. Apparently I'm overdoing it.

LORENE What's happening with Miles and the girlfriend?

FERN They're—serious.

TRICIA   How do you feel about that?

FERN   In the end they do what they want to no matter what
          you say.

          NORMA enters.

NORMA   Hey.

LORENE   Where's Olivia?

NORMA   She's got that flu bug.

LORENE   Seems like we never hear from you girls anymore.

NORMA   Life's busy. How's your back Tissue?

TRICIA   Fine.

LORENE   Hideous.

NORMA   Did you speak to a surgeon?

TRICIA   Yeah. Still fifty-fifty for crippled.

LORENE   Isn't it worth the risk?

TRICIA   I don't know.

FERN   I really don't like seeing you like this.

TRICIA   Me either.

LORENE   Also you're a total bitch.

TRICIA   I know.

OLIVIA *enters.*

OLIVIA   Why the fuck did you leave me at home?

NORMA   You were sleeping.

OLIVIA   You think I'd miss Tish and Lorene's birthday? Fuck that.

NORMA   Did you drive?

OLIVIA   I do have a second set of keys.

FERN   Olivia.

TRICIA   Some flu.

LORENE   You're drunk.

OLIVIA   I'm fine. I came to say happy boiday to my friends even though little miss control here left me asleep on the fucking couch. Is that such a crime?

NORMA   Maybe you should—

OLIVIA   How are you feeling Tissue? Back's not bothering you too much is it?

TRICIA   Actually it is.

OLIVIA   What's to drink? You've got booze right?

LORENE   No.

OLIVIA   I can smell it.

NORMA   Let's go back to the house.

OLIVIA   Fuck off.

LORENE   Olivia.

OLIVIA   You have no right to judge me.

LORENE   Liv stop.

OLIVIA   Aha!

        OLIVIA spots the bottle and pours herself a drink.

NORMA   Please.

OLIVIA   Trish is higher than I am right now.

TRICIA   I am in constant pain.

OLIVIA   So am I. Where's the cake? We're having cake right? Cake and bourbon. Love it.

FERN   You were doing so well.

OLIVIA   Everyone relapses. It's to be expected.

FERN   Livy.

OLIVIA   At least I'm not fucking around on my husband.

LORENE   What?

FERN   You told her?

OLIVIA   She's been fucking the artist next door for like thirty
          years or something.

TRICIA   Seriously?

FERN   You promised you wouldn't tell anyone.

OLIVIA   She has to tell me everything. I'm her wife. Where's
          the goddamn cake.

NORMA   We should just go home.

OLIVIA   When I found out even Fern couldn't keep her mar-
          riage vows I just had to have a drink. Why stay sober
          if everything's a lie right?

FERN   What's a lie?

OLIVIA   Your perfect fucking marriage.

TRICIA   Barry?

LORENE   With the nice legs?

> FERN *takes the bottle from* OLIVIA *and refills her glass.*

FERN   Yes I had an affair. It's over now.

LORENE   Did you tell Walt?

FERN   A few nights ago I'd resolved to say something—we
           were lying in bed—both of us pretending to be asleep
           when he said he'd been having sex with his executive
           assistant for the last five years—

TRICIA   Damn.

FERN   Confessed to the whole messy thing—how young she
           was—how needy she became—how hard it was for him
           to get out of it.

TRICIA   Poor dear.

FERN   He was so sad. He didn't love her. She's gone. He'll
           never see her again.

OLIVIA   So you naturally told him about wiener boy next door.

FERN   No.

LORENE   Really?

FERN   If I'd confessed that I'd done the same thing with Barry
           it would've—I don't know—made it about me. And I

knew deep down this whole thing was about him wanting something—anything—to be about him and not me or the boys or the house or his career or whatever.

NORMA   So what did you do?

FERN   I held him until he fell asleep. And we never talked about it again.

          Pause. OLIVIA pours herself another drink.

OLIVIA   Where's the cake?

LORENE   We were gonna warm up a couple pizzas.

TRICIA   I'm not hungry.

OLIVIA   I'm starving.

NORMA   Let's just go.

          NORMA grabs OLIVIA. OLIVIA pulls away.

TRICIA   Norma.

NORMA   I'm just getting her out of here.

LORENE   Do you have to be so rough?

OLIVIA   She's the one who got me drinking again.

FERN   What?

OLIVIA   Practically poured that cooler down my throat.

NORMA   She said she could handle a drink.

OLIVIA   She likes me when I'm drunk. So she can rub herself
                all over me.

NORMA   Olivia.

OLIVIA   And I can pretend I like it. Just like the bottom did
                with Lorene.

LORENE   Time to shut this party down.

NORMA   Definitely.

OLIVIA   She buys my booze.

NORMA   Olivia we're leaving.

OLIVIA   Still drinking.

TRICIA   You know what a codependent enabler is.

NORMA   Okay. I love an alcoholic.

TRICIA   Why are you killing her?

OLIVIA   I'm great. Don't worry about me.

TRICIA   First do no harm? Isn't that the oath you took?

NORMA   We're leaving.

OLIVIA   No I'm—

> NORMA *grabs* OLIVIA *roughly and hustles her out of the house.*

NORMA   Right fucking now!

OLIVIA   Hey.

> NORMA *drags* OLIVIA *out of the house.*

NORMA   Don't call us again. Any of you.

OLIVIA   Terrible party.

> *They exit. Long pause.*

TRICIA   You should both go now.

FERN   We can still celebrate—

TRICIA   Our failing bodies? Our sham marriages? Our abandoned children?

FERN   My marriage is not a sham.

TRICIA   Well it's not the fabulous success you always pretended it was.

FERN   It's still better than anything either of you have
            achieved.

LORENE   Because you made it last longer by lying?

FERN   I didn't give up my kids.

LORENE   Shut up.

TRICIA   You're both fucking mothers of the year.

LORENE   At least we didn't abort our children.

TRICIA   Fuck you.

FERN   You're a bitter cripple.

TRICIA   You're a lying middle-class bitch.

LORENE   Just stop.

TRICIA   I don't need any of this shit. I never wanted this party
            in the first place. So how about you both fuck off right
            now?

            *FERN and LORENE exit. TRICIA pours herself another
            drink and downs it. Lights rise on NORMA watching
            television. OLIVIA sits next to her drinking.*

OLIVIA   She's fat.

NORMA   What?

OLIVIA   That actress. She's put on weight.

NORMA   Has she?

OLIVIA   I hate this big flat TV. It makes everyone so real.

NORMA   It's fine.

OLIVIA   Let's watch something else.

NORMA   No.

        OLIVIA pours herself another drink, spilling some.

OLIVIA   Aren't you going to clean that up?

NORMA   No.

OLIVIA   Why not?

NORMA   Because I don't want to.

OLIVIA   Well I'm not cleaning it up.

        Pause.

        Why's she wearing that dress?

NORMA   Because it's her husband's favourite and she's planning
          to kill him.

OLIVIA   He should kill her for being so fat and having such bad skin.

NORMA   Stop.

OLIVIA   But wouldn't you agree she's fat. Like fatter than anyone.

NORMA   Sure.

           Pause.

OLIVIA   You wanna drink?

NORMA   I'm trying to watch TV.

OLIVIA   I'm bored.

NORMA   Go to bed.

OLIVIA   That just makes me more bored.

NORMA   Then watch the show.

OLIVIA   She's fat.

           NORMA sighs.

           I'm outta vodka.

NORMA   There's some Tia Maria in the cupboard.

OLIVIA   I hate Tia Maria.

NORMA   It's all we've got.

OLIVIA   Go to the store and get me some more.

NORMA   No.

                     Pause.

OLIVIA   You need to go get me more vodka.

NORMA   No.

                     OLIVIA rises to exit.

OLIVIA   I'll go myself.

NORMA   Don't take the car.

OLIVIA   Whatever.

NORMA   I mean it. Walk.

OLIVIA   Sure.

                     OLIVIA lights a cigarette.

NORMA   And no smoking in the house.

OLIVIA   Don't blame me if I'm raped and murdered.

NORMA   I won't.

OLIVIA   Bye.

> *OLIVIA exits. NORMA slumps in her chair looking like she might cry. There's a sound of a car starting off. NORMA rises and moves to the door.*

NORMA   Olivia?

> *Sound of the car engine being revved and squealing away quickly.*

Fuck.

> *NORMA shakes her head and moves back to her seat to watch television for a moment. The doorbell sounds.*

Yeah?

LORENE   *(off)* It's me.

> *LORENE enters.*

NORMA   Why are you here?

LORENE   Haven't heard from you in a while.

NORMA   Busy.

LORENE   Where's Olivia?

NORMA   What can I do for you Lorene?

LORENE   I thought you might like to come and see Tricia with
         me tomorrow.

NORMA   Why would I want to do that?

LORENE   Because two months ago she could barely walk and was
         the bitchiest person on the planet and now it's like she
         has a whole new lease on life. Just like that. Because
         of one very good surgeon. I know we've all said things
         we can't take back but we are still friends.

NORMA   Are we?

LORENE   Yes. But you're dealing with an alcoholic.

NORMA   Please.

LORENE   Norma. You're miserable.

NORMA   Get out.

LORENE   Okay fine. You just stay here in your dark little house
         that reeks of empty liquor bottles and old lady smells
         and—

         NORMA's communication device rings. NORMA answers it.

NORMA   Yes? What? Is she okay? I see. Which division? Thank
         you.

>*NORMA hangs up.*

LORENE   Division?

NORMA   I have to go.

LORENE   Norma.

NORMA   Fuck off Lorene.

>*NORMA exits. Lights rise on TRICIA at home, seated in a chair.*

TRICIA   It's funny. You get used to pain. You learn to live with it. It's horrible but it also gives you an excuse not to do anything you don't want to. It keeps you constantly aware of what's happening with your body. So when it's suddenly gone—for a while—you actually miss it—like a real cunty friend who drives you crazy but is always there. One day it's the most dominant thing in your life and an operation and a few days later and it's completely gone. But the last thing I expected was a sense of loss.

>*Lights rise on NORMA pacing in a waiting room at the local police station. FERN and LORENE enter. NORMA looks at them balefully and goes on pacing. After a moment TRICIA enters.*

NORMA   Not you too.

TRICIA   Of course.

FERN   Olivia's our friend.

NORMA   Don't.

TRICIA   None of us is going anywhere so get off your high horse
            or I'll have Lorene kick you right in the ass only be-
            cause I can't yet.

            Pause.

FERN   Do you think she'll go to jail?

NORMA   It was a minor accident. No one's going to jail.

LORENE   This is so—low class.

TRICIA   Norma you should've stopped her.

NORMA   I made a mistake okay. I made a mistake and gave her
            a drink because I thought she could handle it. One
            drink. One stupid fucking drink.

LORENE   Norma.

NORMA   I've begged her to stop. You have no idea what's
            she's been like—how bad it's become since she left
            AA. Because she blames me. And she should. It's my
            fault. It is. I was—scared she was going to stop loving
            me—okay stop shut up—don't say it—it is love. It is.
            To me. It's all I know. It's all I ever wanted. I gave up
            everything for her. My family. My friends. I didn't care.
            No one—nothing made me feel as good as when I was

with her and I thought AA was going to take her away and I wanted to stop it but in the end it didn't matter because she doesn't love me. She probably never did.

TRICIA   She does.

NORMA   As a friend. Like a sister. Just like you. Just like everyone because I'm horrible—

FERN   You're nice—

NORMA   I'm not nice. I pretend to be nice so I get what I want. I'm not understanding. I'm not sympathetic—

LORENE   Norma come on.

NORMA   If I'd really loved Olivia I would've put her well-being ahead of my own selfish needs but I didn't want to because I didn't want to be alone. And now she hates me. She's hated me for months—maybe years and so have I. I'm a sad pathetic failure and it's all my fault.

Long pause. LORENE moves to comfort NORMA.

LORENE   Norma it's not as bad—

TRICIA   Don't do it Lorene.

LORENE   What?

TRICIA pushes LORENE away from NORMA.

TRICIA   It's really important we don't negate her responsibility by getting all oh don't worry Norma it's not your fault everything's gonna be alright when it's not.

FERN   Tricia don't be so cruel.

TRICIA   And what'll you say when Olivia does it again and kills someone or hurts herself—it's okay—don't worry about it?

LORENE   She won't do it again.

TRICIA   She's been doing it for years and we've been letting her.

FERN   But she was arrested.

TRICIA   This was a mistake showing up here like this—like we're going to save the day—in some weird way I think she actually gets off on the drama.

FERN   She's our friend.

TRICIA   Booze is her friend.

LORENE   We need to support Norma.

TRICIA   Norma's just as sick as she is. The best thing we can do is walk away and let them figure it out.

LORENE   Trish?

TRICIA   If we don't she'll make us hate ourselves. She'll make us hate each other. Can't you see that? It's happening already. It has been for a while.

FERN   How can you be so mean?

TRICIA   I love them. They're the best friends I've ever had. They get me like no one else ever has. But we can't keep doing this. You both know that.

> *Long pause.*

Good luck Norma.

> *TRICIA exits. Pause.*

LORENE   Call me—if things change.

> *LORENE exits. Pause.*

FERN   Sorry. I'm—sorry.

> *FERN exits quickly. NORMA stands alone. After a moment OLIVIA enters looking terrible. Pause. They stare at one another for a long moment.*

OLIVIA   About fucking time.

NORMA   Don't.

OLIVIA   I was in there for hours.

NORMA   You hit another car.

> *OLIVIA takes the ring off and tosses it on the ground between them.*

OLIVIA   Take your stupid ring.

> *Pause. NORMA exits.*

Norma?

> *OLIVIA moves to the ring and picks it up. A light rises on TRICIA alone.*

TRICIA   It took me about three months to get off the Percocets which isn't too bad considering how addictive they are. My spine healed nicely. I could walk. I started writing again. On the net. I have quite a following and make a bit of money. I've called Norma a few times.

> *A light on OLIVIA.*

OLIVIA   Tissue it's Olivia. I know it's late and everything but I miss you. I really really do. I'm sorry for saying those things but I was drunk—okay I'm always drunk. I'm drunk now. But I miss you. Give me a call. Norma won't talk to me anymore. I'm sorry.

> *A light on LORENE.*

LORENE   Diana had a baby girl. One day I got an email from her and there was a picture of her and this handsome

young man and this beautiful baby girl. No message or
anything. Just a picture. I wasn't sure what it meant—
like if she was being nice or a bitch—but damn that
kid was cute.

The light on OLIVIA *dims.*

OLIVIA   Lorene where the fuck have you been? We're buds remember. Since the third grade. I'm thinking of going
back into AA. I think I have to because they fired me
from my job and Norma's buying a condo. Can you
believe that? She says I can have the house. Fucking
phone me bitch!

FERN *is singled out in a spot.*

FERN   That whole thing about the bride's father paying for
the wedding is really a thing of the past. Actually the
bride had a father and a former stepfather and a cur-
rent stepfather but we still ended up paying the most.
Miles looked so so so manly though in that beautiful
tux. So grown up. Walt cried. I'd never seen him cry
before.

The light on OLIVIA *dims until she is lost in black.*

OLIVIA   Fern it's me. My lights are out. I don't know why. I
sold that ring a few months ago. I sent them money.
There doesn't there isn't I can't I have no power. How
can I have no power? Everything just went out and it's
night. Are you there? Call me if you're there please. I

know it's been a long time but there's this — I'm cold and I have no power. Please call me.

NORMA is singled out in a spot in her new condo. She's going through the ritual of making tea.

NORMA   The view's great. The bedroom's miniscule. I bought a couch that folds out into a guest bed but I never have any guests. I called Tissue a couple times to get together but she was always too busy although we plan to see each other soon and I think we will. Olivia showed up one night and kept screaming up at me from the street. She wanted money for smokes. That was embarrassing but someone eventually told her to shut up or they'd call the cops and she went away. She lost the house. I have trouble sleeping. I always have.

OLIVIA is heard from the darkness.

OLIVIA   Norma!

NORMA pauses almost as if she's heard OLIVIA's distant voice. Pause. A doorbell sounds.

NORMA   Yes?

She opens the door. LORENE, FERN and TRICIA are there. FERN carries flowers.

FERN   Surprise.

Pause.

NORMA   Wow.

FERN   Blame me. When I got your change of address card I called the others and insisted we make a gesture. These are for you.

        FERN hands NORMA the flowers.

NORMA   They're beautiful. Thank you.

LORENE   Won't you ask us in?

NORMA   Of course. Sorry. I was just—surprised. Come in.

        They enter.

LORENE   Thanx.

TRICIA   Not bad.

FERN   It's a wonderful view.

TRICIA   Have you lost weight?

NORMA   A bit.

TRICIA   I could tell.

NORMA   What's new?

LORENE   I'm a grandmother.

FERN   And I'm on my way.

TRICIA   I got a cat.

NORMA   A cat? You were always a dog person.

TRICIA   Cats aren't so obviously codependent.

                The kettle whistles. NORMA *continues to make tea.*

NORMA   You'll all have tea?

LORENE   Sure.

FERN   *(to* NORMA*)* How are you doing?

NORMA   I'm working more. Reading more.

TRICIA   Sleeping more?

LORENE   Sleep is for the young.

NORMA   Thank you for coming by.

FERN   Did you think we wouldn't?

NORMA   Who knows?

LORENE   We go back a long way.

TRICIA   A toast?

FERN   Please.

They all raise their tea cups.

LORENE   Who's going to do it?

NORMA   Tricia.

TRICIA   Sure. To uncertain futures.

THE OTHERS   To uncertain futures.

TRICIA   And absent friends.

A light rises on OLIVIA alone.

THE OTHERS   And absent friends.

OLIVIA   Hello my name's Olivia—and I'm an alcoholic.

Brisk fade to black.

ACKNOWLEDGEMENTS

This play was written with feedback and encouragement from many quarters and it would be remiss of me not to thank the following people: Peni Christopher, Lexa Shropshire, Sharon Vrouwe, Linda Kash, Teresa Tova, Lynne Griffin, Kristina Nichol, Jane Spidell, Shannon McDonough, Maggie Cassella, Lynn Slotkin, Marianne Copithorne, Janice MacDonald, Ali Magnum, Chick Reed, Maria Vacratsis, Colette Leisen, Maryse Warda and all of the other women in my life, and on Facebook, who shared their intimate information with me that contributed to the creation of these characters. Many thanks as well to Sarah Frankcom and the amazing actresses who workshopped the play in London. As always, BJ Radomski, David Gale, Trevor McCarthy and Cameron Conaway must be thanked for their constant feedback and support.

Brad Fraser won his first playwriting competition at the age of seventeen and has since written numerous plays, including *Cold Meat Party*, *Love and Human Remains*, *True Love Lies* and *Poor Super Man*, among others. Brad is a five-time winner of the Alberta Culture Playwriting Competition, a winner of the London Evening Standard Award for Promising Playwright, London's Time Out Award for Best New Play and the L.A. Critics Award. In addition to his work as a playwright and director, Brad writes for print media, radio, film and television.